WITNESS OF FAITH

The Life of Eliza Winn

Nobuo
Umezome

Translated by Komei Kure
Edited by David Rahn and Thomas Charles Winn

Shoraisha Co., Ltd.

Original Japanese Title: *Shinko no Shonin: Eliza Winn den* (New edition)
by Nobuo Umezome
Original Japanese edition published by Kanazawa Church Presbytery, 2007
(Kanazawa Kyokai Chorokai)
English edition published by Shoraisha Co., Ltd., 2020
1-34 Shokakucho, Fushimiku, Kyoto 612-0801 Japan
©2020 Komei Kure, David Rahn, Thomas Chares Winn

Eliza Caroline Winn
(1853-1912)

Thomas Clay Winn
(1851-1931)

HARRISON.   GALESBURG.

The Winn family, circa 1888: Eliza, George, Mary, Julia, Thomas

The Winn family: George, Julia, Merle, Eliza ("Lila"), Mary, Thomas

Author's Foreword to New Edition

The title of this book is *Witness of Faith ~ The Life of Eliza Winn* (New Edition). The original edition was published in May 2003, but was sold out and has been out of print for a while. It is now being republished by the Kanazawa Church Session. I have decided to rewrite the following two points and to publish this edition not as a reprint but revised New Edition. These changes have been accepted by the Church Session.

(1) There were some parts on Christian teaching which deviate quite a bit from the main theme of this book, so in several places these have been simplified or deleted.

(2) In the original edition, the last chapter "Eliza Winn ~Person of Belief" was a summary of an article written by Thomas Clay Winn, since the publication of the original edition, the entire text of the article has been found, so that now the entire text can be found in the Appendix.

I wish to pray to those who will read this book be given joy of salvation as expressed in Hebrews 13:7-8.

"Remember your leaders, those who spoke to you the word of God; consider the outcome of their life, and imitate their faith. Jesus Christ is the same yesterday and today and for ever."

Nobuo Umezome

Preface for the English Edition

I am most delighted that my book *Witness of Faith ~The Life of Eliza Winn* is now translated into English. I would like to express my heartfelt thanks to Professor Komei Kure, who provided the translation, and to David Rahn and Thomas Charles Winn who edited the book. I also would like to extend my deep appreciation to people of the Kanazawa Church who gave me permission to publish this English Edition.

I am now 88 years old, which is called "Age of Rice" in Japanese, as the character "Rice" is composed of numbers 88 written in Japanese characters. Being quite old now, I think of the day when I get to heaven. I hope that on that day I will finally meet Eliza Winn, and will be able to ask her the following question.

"Mrs. Winn, what you did in the Hokuriku District was an amazing achievement. But what was your source of power in this endeavor?"

How would she answer my question? She might answer in this way.

"Mr. Umezome, you know that our source of power is faith in God." Whatever the reply might be, it would be something relevant. What she has done is what God has ordered and that she and her husband Thomas have faithfully achieved.

January 5, 2019

Nobuo Umezome

Introduction
by Thomas Charles Winn

Eliza Willard Winn has left a definite legacy in the education of women in Japan. Yes, she was born into privilege, being a daughter of Silas Willard, a successful merchant. Also, she completed a college education, which was rare for women of her time. Her life coincided with a movement of the era, in which some offspring of affluent families took it to be their duty to go into the far corners of the world and spread Christian teachings. To go to a country like Japan in 1879, a mere ten years after foreigners were first allowed in the country, newly married, and only 27 years old, would have taken extreme faith, courage, and personal flexibility. Thomas, on the other hand, was from a family that was very active in the anti-slavery movement, but he also completed a college education in addition to attending seminary, and had some farming experience.

Mr. Nobuo Umezome, a retired Professor of English from Hokuriku Gakuin Junior College, and an Elder of the Kanazawa Christian Church, has noticed through much research, how strikingly pure the life of Eliza Winn was. As a result, he has written this biography of her life and work in Japan and Manchuria.

This is a translation from Japanese of Mr. Umezome's second, newly revised edition of his book on the subject of Mrs. Winn's life and work. In this book, he makes clear his respect for the example Mrs. Winn set for all of us in terms of hard work and intense efforts to share the teachings of the Gospel with as many people as possible. She was widely known to take every opportunity to guide each person she met toward conversion to the Christian Faith. Beyond this, Eliza found ways to fill nearly every minute of the day with useful effort. She was known for her constant knitting, leaving mittens or socks for the children at each household she visited, also teaching homemaking skills to young women in her spare time.

Mr. Umezome has taken it on himself to create and staff what is called "The Winn Memorial Hall". This is a small museum depicting the work of various missionaries in Kanazawa, including Thomas and Eliza Winn. He staffs this display five days a week, and it is located in the house that Thomas designed and had built on the campus of Hokuriku Gakuin High School. Before this display opened, the building housed a kindergarten for many years, and it is well maintained due to its listing as a Kanazawa City's Cultural Asset.

The Winn and Willard families are very grateful for this collection of research and historical events leading up to Eliza's life, and appreciate knowing of her many accomplishments. As for myself, I am very much in awe of the lives lived by Thomas Clay and Eliza Willard Winn, who were my great-grandparents. My father took me to see Thomas' grave when I was about twelve, and he was a Missionary Professor at Meiji Gakuin University. Much of the family history was completely unknown to me until I was tasked with some of the editing of the English in this book. It is my honor to have met Mr. Umezome, who has been a gracious host to us on several trips to Kanazawa. His commitment to the Christian faith is strong.

Also, I am very much indebted to two of my classmates from Canadian Academy, our high school in Kobe. Komei Kure, professor at Kyoto Seika University (now retired), and David Rahn, were classmates from 1961 to 1964. Komei did the heavy work of the initial translation of this book, and David also helped with the English editing. Komei also translated the book "Thomas Clay Winn-The Life of an American Missionary in Early Modern Japan", which we published in 2004. That book was in its third printing, which was organized by the Kanazawa Christian Church, which was founded by Thomas and Eliza Winn, and was written by a Japanese co-worker of the Winns. It was very heartening to see that the church is complete-

ly independent and self-sustaining and thriving, and that the congregation has built a beautiful new facility, complete with an impressive
French pipe organ. We attended a Sunday service and noticed that
the congregation filled the church. This independence is exactly what
the Winns had hoped for, and continues to this day.

I believe the Winn and Willard descendants will be very pleased
to read this book, since it tells so much about the family history, and
describes Eliza's life so well.

Tom Winn
(Thomas Charles Winn 1945-
2019)

Note by the Translator

Komei Kure

It has been my great delight to translate *Witness of Faith~The Life of Eliza Winn* authored by Mr. Nobuo Umezome in Japanese. Eliza Winn and her husband Rev. Thomas Clay Winn were Protestant missionaries to Japan from 1877 to1906. They served churches in the Hokuriku District, located approximately 360 miles northwest of Tokyo, Japan from 1879 to 1898.

In 2004, I translated *Thomas Clay Winn ～ The Life of an American Missionary in Early Modern Japan*, written by Mr. Shoshichi Nakazawa. This was a book on the great grandfather of Thomas Charles Winn, who had been a classmate of mine at the Canadian Academy High School in Kobe, Japan. I was asked to translate the book so that my classmate's grand-children and relatives would be able to read about the lives and thoughts of their ancestors.

While writing the translation I was much impressed with the account of the life and work of this American missionary couple in early modern Japan. The struggles that they encountered were really severe, particularly in their role of evangelizing Christianity in this remote area of Japan where Buddhism was very strong. I learned that despite these hardships, that Thomas and Eliza Winn had a great impact upon the religious, social, educational, and cultural life of the Hokuriku District.

Translating the book, I realized that Mrs. Winn had played a role equally important to that of her husband in spreading Christianity. She made significant contributions to girls' higher education, kindergarten and elementary education, founding and operating an orphanage, as well as promoting women's activities in the church. I have included the Historical Chart of Hokuriku Gakuin which was developed from the Kanazawa Girl's School that was founded by Eliza and Rev. Thomas Winn. Today Hokuriku Gakuin includes classes from Nursery School to University levels and is all co-educational.

Mr. Nobuo Umezome, the author of the original Japanese text was an English teacher at Hokuriku Gakuin Junior College. He was asked by the School to write about the life of Mary Hesser, the founder of Kanazawa Girls' School. In the course of his study, Mr. Umezome discovered that Eliza Winn was the planner for establishing Kanazawa Girls' School. He has devoted much time in studying the lives of Rev. and Mrs. Winn, and has written a book on both of them. It is so fortunate that Mr. Umezome is active as present director of Winn Memorial Hall at Hokuriku Gakuin, so that I could ask many questions. Mr. Umezome has also provided photographs and other important materials.

I greatly appreciate Mr. Umezome and Kanazawa Church for allowing us to publish *The Life of Eliza Winn*. It was wonderful for me as a translator to be able to visit Kanazawa City recently. It was uplifting to feel the spirit of the work of Rev. and Mrs. Winn, to walk in their footsteps and to witness the legacy of their evangelistic and educational activities. It is my hope that people in Japan, the United States, and elsewhere in the world will read and benefit from this book.

Author's Preface

The title of this book is *Witness of Faith ～ The Life of Eliza Winn.* Eliza Winn is the wife of Thomas C. Winn, an American missionary of early modern Japan. Eliza Winn's maiden name was Willard. Eliza Willard was born to a father involved in business and mother operating a small store. She had been raised in a rather wealthy environment, and was able to attain a high level of education.

Eliza in 1877, soon after graduating from college, married Thomas Winn who had graduated from Union Theological Seminary. She not only went to Japan as the wife of a missionary but as a missionary herself.

Thomas Winn arrived in Kanazawa City, a remote area in the Hokuriku district in northern Japan, and started teaching at the Ishikawa Prefectural Normal School for a Middle School Teachers. This school eventually grew into the Fourth High School, and later on became Kanazawa University. Soon after his arrival, he started the spread of the Christian faith in Kanazawa, by opening the Assembly Hall known as that Nagamachi Kogisho in October 1879.

However, the community of Kanazawa was known historically as an impregnable castle town of the Jodo Buddhist sect. The Buddhist temple began a campaign against Christianity. At that time, Japanese people in general regarded Christianity as a "heathen religion" spread by "barbarous foreigners." There were those at that time who neglected and even abused and persecuted those who preferred Christianity. Under these severe circumstances of persecution, many Christians suffered and died. In spite of the possibility of this harsh suppression, the Winns continued to spread the gospel. As a result, only one year after their arrival, a former samurai of the Kaga Fief confessed his Christian faith, and several other Japanese were baptized. In this way, Kanazawa Church, Tonomachi Church (Kanazawa Motomachi Church), and Toyama Church (Toyama Kashima-cho Church) were founded in the Hokuriku district.

Thomas Winn continued to teach for two years at the Ishikawa Prefectural Normal School. At the end of those two years, the Winns applied to the Prefectural Governor asking for permission to stay longer in Kanazawa, and were given permission to stay and engage in their missionary work. Over the years that the Winns served as missionaries, they also contributed to the welfare of the local people in the following accomplishments:

1. Established and developed the Boys' School.
2. Established and developed the Girls' School.
3. Became involved in saving the lives of the poor.
4. Founded an orphanage for the desperate samurai's children and orphans.
5. Taught skills to members of the church, such as dairy farming, manufacturing western furniture, bicycle repairs and bread baking.
6. Taught women members of the church such skills as western style cooking, knitting wool, the use of sewing machine, manufacturing western clothes and playing the piano and organ.

These activities were all proposed to the local people, and were provided after much discussion. Thomas Winn was responsible for the first and fifth areas of skill. Eliza Winn was responsible for all the rest, numbers 2,3,4 and 6.

In 1898, after 19 years in Kanazawa, the Winns left the Hokuriku district. They transferred to Osaka, and worked there for 8 years. Thomas and Eliza then went on to Dalian, Manchuria, to continue their mission work. But 6 years after arriving there, Eliza had a cerebral hemorrhage and passed away in October 1912, at the age of 59 in Dalian.

For over 35 years, encountering many difficult situations, Eliza loved Thomas, her husband, and worked with him in the mission field. But we need to consider the source of her understanding, and how she was able to whole-heartedly support Thomas' missionary works. Where did she derive the wisdom to raise her four children who then went on to graduate from college? What was the source of her passion to translate a book into Japanese (on John Paton)? How did she develop the leadership skills to manage the activities of a women's group at the Church? What motivated her to engage in social work to help the poor, to establish an orphanage, and take part in other social outreach projects? The author supposes that the source of Eliza's love, understanding, cooperation, wisdom, passion, leadership, and service were rooted in her "belief in the gospel of Jesus Christ".

In the afterword of Life of John G. Paton, which Eliza Winn translated into Japanese, she wrote: "As we become faithful to God, and work for Gospel in endurance, we can be equal to Rev. Paton's deeds and be rewarded greatly at the doomsday of the world."

"To work for Gospel" was like running on the horse track of life. For Eliza, "the Gospel" meant "the power of God for salvation to every one who has faith." (Romans 1:16) With the power of God, Eliza Winn believed that we are all "relieved from the slave of sin in daily life."

Nobuo Umezome

May 2003

CONTENTS

Chapter 1

How Eliza's Father and Mother Met

1. Eliza's family history

Eliza's father was Silas Willard and her mother was Cordelia (maiden name: Chambers). They had one son and 3 daughters, and Eliza was the youngest girl. Eliza Caroline Winn was born on May 1, 1853 in Galesburg, Knox County, Illinois, U.S.A. The following chapter is a brief history of how her parents met and were married, and their move to Knoxville, Illinois.

2. Background of Eliza's father, Silas

Eliza's father Silas Willard was from the State of Vermont. Though the name of the town he comes from is not known, given his occupation and surname, the name of town could be Middlebury, located on the south end of Lake Champlain.

Silas Willard's job was to make horse carriages and harnesses. Middlebury was the main area in Vermont for raising "Morgan horses" which were used for horse carriages and plowing. There was also a market for selling and buying horses. There were few skilled workers who could make harnesses, but Silas was one of them.[1] (A Morgan horse is small and they were popular as work horse. Even today at the University of Vermont's Morgan Horse Farm, 8,500 horses are raised).[2]

Silas' surname Willard provides another clue to where his family

Silas Willard

Cordelia Chambers Willard
(Copyright of photo: Special Collections and
Archives, Knox College Library, Galesburg,
Illinois)

was from. In Middlebury, Vermont, there lived several individuals
with the Willard surname. The most famous of the Willards was Emma Willard (1787-1870).

Emma Willard's ancestry on her father's side extends to Simon
Willard (1605-1676), a Puritan immigrant. Simon immigrated from
Kent, England in 1634, and helped build the City of Concord, Massachusetts Bay Colony. Simon was married three times and had 17
children. Among one of the descendants of Simon, there was Samuel
Willard (1639-1707) who was a Congregational Minister and Vice
President of Harvard College. He himself married twice and had 18
children. Also among Simon's descendants, there was inventor of the
alarm clock, a man who demonstrated outstanding talent and who became famous. Among all his descendants, there was also Simon Willard (1757-1848) having the same name as the original Simon Willard, who was married twice and had eleven children.[3] It is possible
that Emma Willard was an ancestor of Silas.

Matthew Chambers   **Hannah Smith Chambers**

In 1809, Emma married John Willard (1759-1825), a doctor and prominent citizen. She was John's third wife. She established the first secondary girls' school "Troy Girls' Seminary," leading it to become known as an excellent institution. Silas Willard was one of the sons of Emma and John Willard. It is not known how many other children there were from John's previous marriages.

3. Background of Eliza's mother, Cordelia

Eliza's mother Cordelia Willard was the daughter of Matthew Chambers, a businessman. The Chambers were originally Scotch-Irish, belonged to Presbyterian Church and lived in Middlebury, Vermont. Matthew Chambers owned a general store. The store was managed by his wife and employees, and operated a business not only in New England but towns in the Midwest. The store sold a variety of products, including agricultural and construction implements and machines, furniture, clothing, and groceries. Middlebury where

Chambers lived was located in the northern part of the Hudson River Valley, and could be reached from the port of New York. New York was the center of trade, and Middlebury was connected to Boston by wide thoroughfares, travel on foot and horseback was common. At that time, Boston was the center of trade between Europe and New England.

4. Meeting of Silas and Matthew Chambers

The first time that Silas met Matthew Chambers, Cordelia's father, was probably when Silas came to visit Matthew's store on business. Silas was 17 or 18 years old and Matthew was 40 years old.

Matthew Chambers would have ordered harnesses and horse drawn carriages from Silas, and perhaps discussed on the prices of the products. These two men apparently talked in friendly tones. After the business transaction took place, these two men talked about current issues affecting the United State.

The topics were varied. They talked over the European countries and war, disputes with native Americans, issue on slaves, harnesses and horse carriage, varieties of machinery and new products. At this point, Silas would have been more of the listener. He was amazed at the wide knowledge of Mr. Chambers based on his rich experiences, and the information on U.S. and European discoveries and inventions. For Silas who had never gone outside his community, this was a big surprise. While talking to Silas, Matthew Chambers got to like this young man. Silas listened to Matthew Chambers intently, and saw that he behaved in a polite and courteous manner in speaking to his elders.

Meanwhile, the harnesses that Silas had made were displayed at Chambers' store. Soon after this, Silas was offered to a position at Chambers' store. Silas quite quickly adapted to the new job and environment. Along with his knowledge, skills, and experiences with horse carriages and harnesses, his sincere and frank personality made a positive impression on customers. Silas developed a positive reputation and was soon trusted by the Chambers' family.

5. Chambers going to Illinois

Matthew Chambers often travelled across Lake Champlain, going down the Hudson River and then to New York. From there, riding on horse carriage going around Appalachian Mountains, he reached Buffalo, a trade city located on Lake Erie. On the way to New York going 150 kilometers northwest, Matthew Chambers rested in a town called Middletown. Near this town, there was a small village named Whitesboro, and there existed a Christian school. The school was called Oneida Institute of Science and Industry, and George Gale, Presbyterian pastor and educator operated an institution gathering students not able to support themselves financially. Students made a commitment to working on the farm to support themselves financially. They were provided textbooks and taught general subjects and electives. They were also offered classes such as theology and reading the Bible in classical languages.

Around 1833, Matthew Chambers heard the following story in the town of Middletown. It was that President George Gale of Oneida Institute of Science and Industry was planning to develop his educational ideal and establish a huge institution "Prairie College" in the Midwest, and build a college town, where the railway was to be extended from Chicago. The plan was to build the college near Knoxville, Illinois. This became an attractive opportunity for Matthew Chambers.[4]

6. Actual Survey of Knoxville

Matthew Chambers immediately went all the way to Illinois with Silas Willard to do an actual survey of Knoxville. Silas had by that time become his right-hand man in business. There was a town named Pekin along the Illinois River, and this place seemed to be a perfect site to operate a general store. Most of the people in this town had moved westward around 1820's from northeastern New England, searching for rich and reasonably priced land, and most of them belonged to the Congregational Church. In Knoxville, there was no such store as a "Chambers' Store". Matthew Chambers and Silas Willard both thought, "If there were a store selling miscellaneous goods, it would be convenient for villagers and they will be glad to have it."

Then, Matthew Chambers and Silas Willard looked over the prospective land where the "Prairie College" and college town was to be built.

"If direct railway is connected from Chicago and Aurora in the east, Burlington on the west, and neighboring Kansas, the college and college town will develop for sure," and they thought the future was bright.

7. Moving of Chambers and marriage of Silas and Cordelia

There was an important matter that Matthew Chambers pondered and discussed with his wife. The matter was that Chambers would move their family home to a Midwestern or western town. In those days many from New England States and even those from near-by Vermont towns, emigrated to the Midwest and further to the California gold mines. For them, it was "the problem of possibilities." Matthew Chambers had in mind to move to Pekin and Knoxville. Furthermore, he imagined the future of a college and college town appearing in the Prairie. Finally, he decided to immigrate and he consulted his family and asked for their support.

However, aside of loneliness to move out from their community, there was the joyous event of a wedding. Matthew's daughter Cordelia and Silas got married and the couple had their wedding at Middlebury Church in Vermont. The wedding ceremony was not elaborate but solemn. All the villagers gathered together and blessed the newly wed couple.

It was the spring of 1834. Chambers departed and said farewell to the people of Middlebury, leaving Vermont where they have lived so long, and headed for Illinois. Silas and Cordelia went to Illinois with Matthew and his wife Hannah. As soon as they reached Illinois, Matthew Chambers opened a general store in the town of Pekin. He had Silas and Cordelia look after the store. From this time on, Silas was part of the management team of Chambers' chain stores. Matthew opened another store in Knoxville and had his wife Hannah manage it. There were also a few employees who moved from Middlebury to be with them.

8

Chapter 2

George Gale's "The Prairie College"

1. The Naming of Knox College

Founded by George Gale, Knox College was first named "The Prairie College." The name was derived from the fact that the State of Illinois is widely known as "The Prairie State." The State of Illinois is located in the Midwest with its northeastern area facing Lake Michigan. The second largest trade and industrial city of the United States, Chicago is located in Illinois on the southwest corner of Lake Michigan. Composed of 102 counties, the state became the twenty-first State of the Union in 1818. Illinois is called "The Prairie State" because it is blessed with rich prairie soil which is favorable to growing corn, wheat and soybeans. Products related to the raising of cattle and pigs became important. Illinois is also rich in underground resources including coal, oil and non-ferrous metals. This led to the development of the manufacturing, farming implements, machines in general, pharmaceutical chemicals, as well as steel manufacturing.

In 1834, Eliza's grandfather and grandmother, Matthew and Hannah Chambers, moved from Vermont and opened a store in Knoxville, a village of agriculture and dairy farming. The origin of the name "Knox" appearing in "Knoxville" and "Knox County" is derived from General Henry Knox (1750-1806), with the suffix "ville" indicating village or town. When George Washington was inaugurated as the first President of the U.S., Henry Knox was promoted to General of the Northern Army from Artillery leader due to his accomplishments.

However, the Knox of "Knox College" differs in origin from these local sources. George Gale who originally named the college "The Prairie College" after the nickname given to the state of Illinois, later decided to reference the name of John Knox the Scottish religious reformer whom he had studied, adopted and followed.

2. George Gale

The town Eliza grew up in was Galesburg, which means "Town of Gale." The name is derived from the person who had conceived the idea of building the town. George Washington Gale (1789-1861) came from New York. His father was an immigrant from York, England. His mother came from Connecticut, the state adjoining New York. George Gale graduated from Union College. Following college graduation, he suffered from illness for 5 years. He later recovered from this illness, and studied at Princeton Theological Seminary affiliated with the Presbyterian Church. He then became the pastor of a church in Adams, New York.

In 1824 Gale resigned as pastor due to illness, and spent time reading on rainy days, working outside on sunny days. During that time, he came up with an idea of making an educational institution of higher learning "Working and studying Theology at the same time." At that time, pastors well versed in theology were rare, and it was because young men and women could not afford financially to study theology.

George Gale established a small experimental school in Whitesboro, and for 7 years following 1827, became head master and manager of the school. During this period he prayed to God and planned that a college based on his ideal would become true.

3. Religious belief of Charles Finney

George Gale was a minister in the state of New York, and Charles

Finney happened to be an assistant pastor at George Gale's Church. Charles Grandison Finney (1792-1875) was from Connecticut and was originally a schoolteacher. He then became a lawyer, but at the age of 29, he had a soul-shaking conversion experience. After serving 3 years as apprentice pastor, Charles became a Presbyterian preacher. Thereafter for 8 years, he engaged in revival gatherings on the east coast. He attained great success, and later was called the "Father of the Christian Revival Movement in the Modern Age."

Lyman Beecher (1775-1863) was one of many influenced by Finney at a New York gathering. Beecher was the father of Mrs. Stowe, who was the author of Uncle Tom's Cabin. Beecher later became an eloquent preacher. A revival movement led by Finney and Beecher was called "The Second Great Awakening". According to Mary B. Norton et al.: *A People and a Nation*, this movement is described as follows:

> The Second Great Awakening also raised people's hopes for the Second Coming of the Christian messiah and the establishment of the Kingdom of God on earth. Revivalists set out to speed the Second Coming by creating a heaven on earth. They joined the forces of good and light—reform—to combat those of evil and darkness. Some revivalists even believed that the United States had a special mission in God's design, and therefore a special role in eliminating evil. [1]

4. Is religious belief reason or emotion?

Finney and Beecher represented Presbyterian and some Congregational pastors, for whom the Religious Revival Movement was called the "Second Religious Reconstruction Movement." From the late 17th through the 18th centuries, the "Great Awakening" occurred in the Northern and Southern colonies. This movement was called the "First Religious Reconstruction Movement", which focused on spiritual experience as being the proper method in attaining faith. The Movement disregarded religion without spiritual elevation, and led to internal conflicts in the Presbyterian and Congregational Churches.

George Gale expressed the opinion that faith should not be replaced by emotions. However, he insisted that reason is not the only source of knowledge and that believers should not rely on what was called "Deism". His understanding was very close to the German Reformist Nevin, who was a pastor and theologian. John Nevin (1803-1886) criticized the elevation of belief and pointed out that not faith but emotion overpowers, and for spiritual elevation that educational preaching was important – focusing on real spiritual experience and with an emphasis on the importance of Holy Communion and rituals.[2]

Chapter 3

The Founding of Knox College

1. The founding of College

George Gale is credited with being the first to propose the establishment of what would become the "Prairie College". The historian, Elmo Calkins, provided in 1827 the following account of "The Goals for establishing Prairie College:" The book on the goals for the college was written with a certain dignity. The purpose of the college was to be as follows:

> It continues in the same strain, pointing out the duty of creating ministers to save our political institutions from falling into the hands of "those who are no less enemies of civil liberty than of pure gospel"; demonstrating that the manual-labor system "is peculiarly adapted to qualify men for the self-denying and arduous duties of the gospel ministry, especially in our new settlements and missionary fields abroad," and with a diplomatic touch, mindful of the wives who will read this appeal over their husbands' shoulders, he makes a handsome concession to woman's sphere: "It is beginning to be believed that females are to act a more important part in the conversion of the world than has generally been supposed, not as preachers," he hastens to add, "but as helpmates to those who are." [1]

2. The goal of the College, and maintaining its belief system

"Prairie College" at the time of its establishment was named "Knox Manual Labor College," which was later changed into "Knox Col-

Knox College which Eliza attended

lege." The name Knox is derived from the Scottish religious reformer, John Knox. George Gale wished that the theology of John Knox
would be the founding spiritual and educational goals of the college.

The belief system and theology that George Gale accepted in those
days was called "hyper-Calvinism." Charles Finney, who was a follower of John Knox, but occasionally his rival, adhered to it. Finney
in his writing described the importance to him of George Gale's
thinking, and its connection to John Calvin's "Belief in the Gospel
according to Jesus Christ."

3. Belief of the religious reformers

The "Belief in the Gospel" has its roots in the reformers Luther,
Calvin, and Knox. There were significant differences in the beliefs of
this line of reformers. But the developments of their beliefs follow a
similar pattern, and their work led to the founding of Knox College.

Martin Luther had tried to center the Gospel of the Bible as the basis of Christian faith, and began to promote reform against certain contemporary practices of the Catholic Church. The three principles he had set up for religious reforms were:

(1) "Faith alone": People will be saved only by faith.

(2) "Bible alone": the Bible is the sole foundation of faith, and has utmost authority.

(3) "All people are ministers" All believers are ministers of God.

John Calvin was the leader of the religious reformation in Geneva and other major cities in Switzerland. The core of his theology was "God centeredness." He emphasized "Faith alone" among Luther's three principles of religious reformation, denied secular power and resisted Catholic practices as well as some of Luther's other beliefs. His theology emphasized "predestination," that some by God's will would be eternally saved, and that others eternally condemned. He organized his Church using what was then called the presbyter system, and demanded strict discipline in both public and private lives. His theology was put forward in *The Institute of Christian Religion* and *The Catechism of the Church of Geneva.* [2]

This Reformed Presbyterian Church became the Huguenot movement in France. Its followers moved northward along the Rhine River and founded reformed churches. In Holland they established the "Dutch Reformed Church," and in England they founded "Puritanism." Moving on to Scotland the movement became the Scottish Church.

John Knox was the leader of the religious reformation in the Scottish Church. After coming under Calvin's influence in Geneva, he worked to found the Presbyterian Churches. The Parliament of Scotland at that time amended the "Scottish Creed," and Knox then turned his attention to reforming the Presbyterian churches in Scotland. Knox also criticized the Catholic faith of Queen Mary Stuart of England, and promoted religious reform.

John Knox described the importance of believing in what he calls the genuine Gospel in his work, "The Scottish Confession, " and emphasized in his preface, "Inheriting faith."

> We declare that if there are those who find some words and phrases contradicting the God's holy words in this confession of Faith, that such people should notify the authors with Christian faith and love by writing out their concerns. We remain in honor and truth, speaking from God's words. The Bible will refute the doubts, or correct inappropriate words, either will be promised. And we earnestly and humbly insist on preaching the Gospel according to Christ. The genuine Gospel must be highly valued and should not be diminished. We must be determined to overcome the greatest danger in the world. [3]

Founded by Knox's reformation, Scotland's Presbyterian Church became the foundation of the Presbyterian Church, spreading throughout the U.S.A. and through Ireland. One of the Scotch Irish Presbyterians, Francis Makemie, established the Philadelphia Presbytery. With the formation of the Philadelphia Synod (a regional organization of individual churches), Makemie in 1789 organized the First National General Meeting of the U. S. Presbyterian Church. Due to the divisive issue of slavery that led to the subsequent Civil War, the church was divided into Northern and Southern presbyteries.

4. The Administration policy of the College

The following statement appeared in the "Application to establish a College," the summary of administration policy, presented to the Federal and Illinois state governments.

(1) Of the 465,920 acres of land owned by government in Knox County, 23,040 acres (@$1.25 per acre) were to be purchased. Due to the shortage of fund holders, only 12,800 acres were acquired.

(2) The College would use 1,920 acres for its campus, with the remaining land sold to individuals 1 lot (80 acres @$5.00 per acre). The profit from the sale of this property and subtracting

the cost of campus land was to be allotted to a 25 year-loan for student scholarships.

(3) Besides the profit from the sale of the land, donations of $40,000 were to be raised. The college facilities and institutions including a chapel, athletic field, and farm were to be built with these funds.

5. From the initial concept of the establishment of the College to its actual opening

George Gale had the initial concept of the "Prairie College" as early as 1827. But it wasn't until 1841 that the college was finally established. The many ways that the college and the college town changed during this time can be best described by observing the relationship of Chambers and Willard's activities to historical events:

(1) 1827   George Gale announced the idea of building a college.

(2) 1830   The Baltimore and Ohio Railways started its operation.

(3) 1831-38 The "Trails of Tears': Native Americans were forced to move to the west of the Mississippi River.

(4) 1834   The Board of the College was formed, and the educational foundation established, and was accredited by the State Government.

(5) 1834   Abraham Lincoln was elected as a Senator representing Illinois.

(6) 1834   Silas Willard opens a general store in the town of Pekin.

(7) 1834   Matthew Chambers opens a store in Knoxville.

(8) 1835   At the meeting of an ad hoc committee of the First Presbyterian Church in Rome, New York, it was decided that a $700 salary be paid to George Gale.

(9) 1835   A Committee was formed for establishing a College, and Knox County was designated as the location of the new campus.

(10) 1836   George Gale came to inspect Knox County in person.

(11) 1836   Matthew Chambers and other people met George Gale, and Chambers purchased 1 lot of land.

(12) 1836   Donations were raised gradually, with a number of advance purchases.

(13) 1837   The founding of Knox Manual College was approved by the Illinois legislature.

(14) 1837   The Galesburg Presbyterian Church and its Elementary School began occupancy of the new buildings constructed by Matthew Chambers (including an adjoining residence, workshop and store complex).

(15) 1837   The Nationwide Financial Panic of 1837

(16) 1837   Matthew Chambers was appointed as a Board member of Knox College.

(17) 1838   Construction of the College buildings started

(18) 1839   Some College buildings were completed, and preparatory education for entering college was started.

(19) 1841   The women's building was completed; a portion of the farm-land was ready for use, and regular courses and research activities were begun.

The population of Galesburg in 1837 was 173, and in the following year, increased to 232. It was a rather small town, and most of the people were engaged in farming, and lived in the "log cabin district" away from the center of town. With all of these problems, George Gale and his associates believed that they needed to pray to God to find support for their vision. They have done all that they could to accomplish their educational goals. From 1839 a preparatory course was started for a small group of youngsters wishing to study, and college education classes started in 1841.

George Gale had come up with the concept of the "Prairie College" in 1827. His prayers for the establishment of the college continued for fifteen years, until finally in 1841 the college was founded. When Gale and his associates started the college, there was a three-story building for female students. Beyond this building was a vast farmland.

6. Prayers were heard and miracles occurred

There were many hurdles to clear in those early years. It was challenging to gain acceptance for the idea of the college that was only a place "to work and study at the same time, but that was coeducational as well." The United States at that time was going through a political "colonial period," and entering the religious "age of reformation." There was big flow of immigrants who had an important role in opening up and cultivating the prairie. Slave issues in the south, the shift to a new political system, repeated financial panic, the confusions created by the gold rush of 1849, the building of high-cost transcontinental railways, and many other problems arose with the building of a new nation. Moreover, the Civil War was about to begin splitting the nation into two.

A quotation from Earnest Calkins, historian, has been cited at the beginning of this chapter. The book quoted has the title *They Broke the Prairie*, and reminds us of Exodus 14:1~31 "The miracle of the Reed (Red) Sea."

> Then Moses stretched out his hand over the sea; and the Lord drove the sea back by a strong east wind all night, and made the sea dry land, and the waters were divided. And the people of Israel went into the midst of the sea on dry ground, the waters being a wall to them on their right hand and on their left. The Egyptians pursued, and went in after them into the midst of the sea, all Pharaoh's horses, his chariots, and his horsemen. And in the morning watch the Lord in the pillar of fire and of cloud looked down upon the host of the Egyptians, and discomfited the host of the Egyptians, clogging their chariot wheels so that they drove heavily; and the Egyptians said, "Let us flee from before Israel; for the Lord fights for them against the Egyptians.
>
> Then the Lord said to Moses, "Stretch out your hand over the sea, that the water may come back upon the Egyptians, upon their chari-

ots, and upon their horsemen." So Moses stretched forth his hand over the sea, and the sea returned to its wonted flow when the morning appeared; and the Egyptians fled into it, and the Lord routed the Egyptians in the midst of the sea. The waters returned and covered the chariots and the horsemen and all the host of Pharaoh that had followed them into the sea; not so much as one of them remained. But the people of Israel walked on dry ground through the sea, the waters being a wall to them on their right hand and on their left. (Exodus 14:21~29)

Chapter 4

Father as Businessman and Mother as "A Woman of Prudence"

1. Eliza's Father's contribution in railroad construction

This chapter will focus on the work of Eliza's parents, Silas and Cordelia Willard. Emphasis will be on their work from 1841, when "The Prairie College" was founded, through 1854, when the railroad was constructed as far as Galesburg.

To begin with, Eliza's father, Silas Willard, had made a reputation in building the Kansas Pacific Railroad. This railroad was to become part of the American transcontinental railroad. Had not Silas supplied the funds, and provided materials and implements, the east and west coasts would not have been joined and the United State would not have been joined together.

The population of Galesburg in 1850 was 882. It was anticipated that funds would be available to build the railroad as far as the town. The railroad had reached Aurora, Illinois which was 70 kilometers southwest of Chicago. It was 220 kilometers from Aurora to Galesburg. The cost of purchasing the railroad Right of Way, however was set at $400,000 and the builders were short $150,000. The deadline for payment was fast approaching when two young businessmen, Chauncey Colton and Silas Willard provided the funds.

And so the railroad construction started. Colton and Willard became members of the board of the railroad company and played im-

House built by Eliza's father Silas Willard in 1856-57. Address: 501 East Losey St. Galesburg, Illinois (Presently used as Guest House)

portant roles in completing the railroad project. Both of them at great personal expense were involved in the project. It took more than 4 years. Immense amounts of money and labor were needed. But construction was completed in 1854. Finally the railroad reached Galesburg.

The effect of the railroad construction was seen immediately. The enrollment of "The Prairie College" gradually increased. Two new college buildings were built, and stoves were installed in the classrooms. Agricultural and dairy products were transported to distant markets, and the trains brought back everyday convenience goods. Those in business could travel quickly and for great distances. The population of Galesburg in 1846 was 800, but by 1856 it had increased to 4,000.

2. Chambers' "woman of prudence"

Mrs. Eliza Winn once said to the church people of Dalian, Manchuria that: "My mother was the woman who owned the Chambers' general store in Knoxville, Illinois and was called 'A woman of prudence'." "Prudence" according to the dictionary means "intelligent and sound judgment, careful in thought in coping with actual problems. It is derived from the word "providence." The original meaning is "to foresee things that are ahead."

The change in society and economy was reflected in the changing role of women. Men and women traditionally had clearly distinguishable work roles. The work of women had for many years centered on the family. As the family lost its identity in manufacturing products in private homes, maintaining a household and raising children became their main role. Women had been involved in these manufacturing activities all day long. The family was no longer a unit of production, so that education, religion, morals, handcrafts, and maintaining the culture of the community became the primary role of women. This role of family management was called "the proper role of women" or "the cult of domesticity of the nineteenth century, " and was held to be the ideal role of women.[1]

Eliza's mother, Cordelia was more than one of the "women" described previously. She not only managed to establish a fine family environment, but also was able to manage the store that her husband handed over to her. She could manage the employees and supply the people of Knoxville with necessary daily goods. Moreover, she led a gathering of women either at her home or at Galesburg Presbyterian Church. She was part of social exchanges, and had organized the "Little Band of Associated Females," which came out of the "Faith Reconstruction Movement." This band of "Females" supported the educational activities of the elementary school, supported institutions helping children, and gathered offerings for the missionary work of the Presbyterian Women's Mission. Indeed, Cordelia Chambers well deserves to be called "A wise woman of prudence."

3. A Chronology of the years 1841-54

How Eliza's father Silas' business activities and her mother Cordelia's social involvements were reflected in world events.

(1) 1841: Education begins at "The Prairie College"

(2) 1848: Illinois State's New Constitution was approved, and the abolition of slavery was clearly stated.

(3) 1848: Canal joining Illinois and Michigan completed and Great Lakes and Mississippi River were connected.

(4) 1848: "Women Rights" were declared at Seneca Falls, New York.

(5) 1849: Silas Willard opens general store in Galesburg.

(6) 1850: Silas Willard and other people provide funding for railroad constructions between Aurora and Galesburg, and construction was started.

(7) 1852: Mrs. Stowe publishes *Uncle Tom's Cabin*, and this first year 300,000 copies were sold.

(8) 1853: Eliza was born as the third daughter of the Willards.

(9) 1854: Railroad reaches Galesburg and is connected to the Mississippi River.

Chapter 5

The Gift of Encounter

1. Birth, naming, and infant baptism

Eliza Willard was born on May 1, 1853. How Eliza —called "Lila" as a child—got her nick-name is not known. A few days after Eliza's birth, her parents would have probably asked the pastor of the Galesburg First Presbyterian Church to baptize their baby. Many who believe in the Christian faith accept the significance of "the gift of encounter." For Lila and her family, it would be the moment when Lila

Eliza in teens

and her family could tell that she had experienced an encounter with Jesus Christ. There was nothing to hinder this encounter. The words "we confess and understand" appear in Chapter 23 of "The Scottish Confession." It is thought to be a right for both children and adult believers of the church to receive baptism.[1] Lila received infant baptism but in order to be able to receive Holy Communion when she attended adult's service, she asked the church and confessed her belief. The detail of the confession will be stated in Chapter 8. Concerning baptism, a segment of the Congregational and Baptist Churches do not accept infant baptism.

2. Experience of "the Pain of hot flames"

Lila always attended Sunday School. (today it is called Church School) every Sunday morning. Lila's parents as well as everyone else in the family attended church services to pray to God. This was the custom of the Willard family. A member of Dalian Japanese Christian Church in Manchuria wrote a book called *The Life of Mrs. Winn*. In this book an episode is recounted of Lila around 5 to 6 years old , putting her hand in a burning furnace and yet not getting burned. This experience can be summarized as follows.

Beating within the young heart of Lila there were strong images. The first was the image of a Christian cross, which had a powerful impact on her thinking for her entire life. The second was the disaster that befell the apostle Paul. The child Lila wondered how far a person of faith could be able to endure the pain, and so attempted to discover an answer for herself when nobody was at home. She apparently put her hand in the flame of the furnace, trying to experience the "suffering of the burning flame." This event might be seen from the point of view of the mental disposition and impulsiveness of a child. But perhaps it can be seen as a sign of faith that she would serve God and later commit herself to a life-time of missionary work abroad.[2]

Eliza Winn most likely talked about this episode later in her life.

The author of *The Life of Mrs. Winn* has written that strange as her actions may seem to us today, the motive for her action was derived from "Paul's disaster." There is also the possibility that young Lila was influenced by readings from Mark 9:44-46, as well Isaiah 33:14, Daniel 3:1-30 in the Old Testament. It is possible that Lila could have been influenced by the story in book of Daniel of the "Believer who has been thrown into the burning furnace but was saved." Stories from the Bible were often read in Sunday Schools. In the Book of Daniel, there is the well known story of Daniel being saved after being thrown into the lion's den.

3. Story of "Shadrach, Meshach and Abednego saved from fire"

The Book of Daniel was written in response to the reign of the new King of Syria Antiocos Epiphonus. When he became king he began to ridicule the shrines of Israel and repeatedly tormented them for their beliefs. The author of Daniel Chapter 1-6 used a story format that was popular during the time of the persecution of Antiocos. The Book of Daniel was written in order to provide comfort and encouragement for the Jewish people.

In the story of the fiery furnace (Daniel 3), Daniel and three of his friends Shadrach, Meshach and Abednego were taken as captives to Babylon. King Nebuchadnezzar had a figure of gold created, and ordered his people to worship it. But Daniel's three friends Shadrach, Meshach and Abednego refused to pray to the image. The king was angered that the three friends ignored his authority. He had Shadrach, Meshach and Abednego tied up and thrown into the burning furnace, telling them, "Your God cannot save you." Much to the king's astonishment, God gave Shadrach, Meshach, and Abednego protection from the flames. Although the rope was torn away, and burnt, Shadrach, Meshach and Abednego did not have any severe wounds, and survived the ordeal. The king was astonished at the miracle that took place in front of him. He ordered Shadrach, Meshach and Abednego to be brought out from the furnace, and then issued a proclamation to his people that

> Any people, nation, or language that speaks anything against the God of Shadrach, Meshach, and Abednego shall be torn limb from limb, and their houses laid in ruins; for there is no other god who is able to deliver in this way. [Daniel 3:29]

4. Meeting Winn's family

Lila would have been about five years old in the spring of 1858 when she first met young Thomas Winn and his family at Sunday School. The two families would become close to each other, and years later Thomas and Lila would marry. He was thin and not very tall. He was one or two years older than Lila, but was rather weak and could not engage in strenuous activities. Thomas could have been considered " at first glance an unattractive boy." Thomas' father taught Christianity at Knox College. Also his father was a minister and happened to preach occasionally at the Galesburg Presbyterian Church. Lila most likely became a bit curious about Thomas.

A few days after Lila's first meeting Thomas, his "famous grandmother" came to Galesburg. She was the grandmother of Thomas and came to Galesburg from New York State to be with the family. The name of his grandmother was Phoebe Brown, and she was over 70 years old. She happened to be a well known author of hymns and poetry. She moved in with Thomas' aunt next door to Thomas' home. Grandmother Brown soon became well known in Galesburg.

Every Sunday the Willards attended the same church as the Winn family. The Winn and Willard families belonged to the Presbyterian Church which was influenced by the Reformist theology of Calvin and Knox.

Chapter 6

Days as an Elementary School Pupil, Lincoln, and the Civil War

1. A clever girl

Eliza (or Lila she was called), was in elementary school from 1860 through 1867, from when she was 7 until she was 14 years old. By the 1830's the Illinois State Legislature had passed a law that all children regardless of gender must receive an Elementary education. The "Illinois State Education Law" stating that an elementary education must be provided free was passed in 1848. The population of Illinois was a mixture of those from both Northern and Southern States. The state adopted regulations from both regions. The law for establishing tuition free schools and a levy system was established, and fees were optional. The traditional system in Illinois also allowed for a "rate bill," in which payment by wealthy families supported the running of the school system. Lila's parents paid an education fee which allowed children study at school.[1]

At the school Lila attended, she learned reading, writing, arithmetic, history, and geography (especially concentrated on the countries of Greece, Rome, England, Scotland, and the United States.) Lila did very well in all subjects. The subjects Lila particularly liked were reading, writing, and history.

Lila was a clever girl. She was intelligent, knowledgeable, and witty. Her mother Cordelia could always talk with pride of Lila's accomplishments when she met with her women's group.

2. Stories told by grandfather

Lila's grandfather Matthew Chambers was a strong believer in Calvinism. He lived in the neighboring town of Knoxville, and had his hardware store operated by his wife and his employees. He engaged in other business handling construction tools, farming equipment and all necessary daily products in the Midwest and along the East coast. However, he just only made a small margin of profit, in one instance making $3.25 in a business dealing of a few hundred dollars. His business approach was very reasonable. He had been on the Board of Trustees of Knox College for a long time until 1888, and contributed a great deal in education and for society.

Lila loved her grandfather. Matthew loved her as well. The grandfather enjoyed every time he came to Galesburg to see Lila. Her grandfather told Lila about his early memories of Vermont surrounded by woods. He shared with Lila his earlier memories about Emma Willard, cousin of Lila's father Silas, who organized the first seminary for women in U.S.A. He also shared his concern that America would split into North and South over the slave issue, and his view that probably a war would occur.

3. Illinois and Lincoln

The period while Lila was elementary school was called the "Age of Turmoil." From his origins in the State of Illinois, Lincoln became President of the United States. And it was during this period the Civil War was fought.

Abraham Lincoln (1808-1865) was born in a log cabin in Kentucky. Later, his family in the wave of frontier settlement, moved first to Indiana, and then to Illinois, eventually settling in Illinois. Lincoln did not receive a formal education, but was self-taught. He worked at various jobs including making rafts, rowing boats, carpentry, butcher, a mountain ranger, clerk, liquor manufacturer, farmer, and director of the post office. In 1834 he became involved in the state government of Illinois, becoming a member of the State House of Representatives. Meanwhile he studied law on his own, and became a lawyer in 1837 in Springfield, Illinois, the State Capital. From 1841 through 1845, he became a member of the Congressional House of Representatives. In 1858, knowing that Stephen Douglas was planning to propose a bill defending slavery as a Democratic representative, Lincoln rose up to run as a Republican Senator, and debated Douglas seven times on this issue. These Lincoln and Douglas debates became famous in U. S. history.

The 5th Lincoln-Douglas Debates took place at the Knox College campus in Galesburg. An audience of about 15,000 gathered. In Chapter 3 of this book, there is a photo of Knox College where the debate took place here. Lila might very well have attended to see this scene and would have seen the 190 cm(6 ft. 4 in.) "tall Lincoln" even from a distance.

Most of the people in Galesburg had come originally from Northwestern New England. There were a few black people living in town, hired by wealthy families and stores, but there were no slaves living in Galesburg. If Lila had seen Lincoln she would have been only five years old. Perhaps even at that young age, Lila would have understood that there were many black people who were slaves in the South who were forced to work as though they were cattle and horses, and not living as ordinary citizens.

4. Civil War

America experienced the biggest and most horrible internal war in its history when Lila was between the ages of 8 and 12. At that time in the North, industry developed and favored protective trade, and was against slavery. On the other hand, the South was greatly dependent on cotton cultivation and insisted on free trade and slavery. So the socio-economic interests of North and South contradicted each other. Finally, a spark ignited this conflict into war. Lincoln lost to Douglas in the debates, but went on to become President of the United States in 1860. Seven Southern States had declared to secede from the Union, but Lincoln as the new President opposed them, and in 1861 the Civil War broke out. Lincoln eventually proclaimed the "Declaration of the Emancipation of Slaves" in 1863, and this became part of the war to end slavery. In November of that same year, Lincoln gave his monumental "Gettysburg Address," and the following year, was reelected President. The Civil War finally ended as the Southern Army surrendered in April 1865.

Lila would have heard much about the War. The North had twice as many soldiers as the South for example, and many had volunteered from Knox County to fight for Lincoln and the Northern Army. It was true that one-third of the soldiers of the South were slaves, that many slaves run away to refuse to become soldiers. There were also brave women who worked in the battlefield to help provide medical treatment and take care of wounded soldiers. Lila was a delicate and sensitive girl, and all this would have been very hard for her emotionally.

5. Lincoln and Christian Faith

Soon after the Civil War ended, the entire country was astonished at hearing the news. Five days after the end of the Civil War, an assassin shot Lincoln while he was in a theater.

Lila's Sunday School teacher talked about Lincoln and the Bible and mourned his death. Before becoming the President, Lincoln was very busy and couldn't have gone to attend church services. However, over the course of the Civil War over a period of about 4 years, Lincoln's Christian faith deepened. According to Paul Johnson's *History of the American People,* Lincoln's religious state of mind is described as follows:

> His evident and total sincerity shines through all his words as the war took its terrible toll. He certainly felt the spirit of guidance. "I am satisfied," he wrote "that when the Almighty wants me to do or

not to do a particular thing, he finds a way of letting me know it.".... He never claimed to be the personal agent of God's will, as everybody else seemed to be doing. But he wrote: "If it were not for my firm belief in an overriding providence it would be difficult for me, in the midst of such complications of affairs, to keep my reason in its seat. But I am confident that the Almighty has his plans and will work them out; and...they will be the wisest and the best for us....Early in the war, a delegation of Baltimore blacks presented him with a finely bound Bible in appreciation of his work for the negroes. He took to reading it more and more as the war proceeded, especially the Prophets and the Psalms.... As he told the Baltimore's blacks: "This great Book...is the best gift God gave to man."[2]

What her Sunday School teachers taught as "firm confidence in God's providence," and the words of Lincoln that the Bible is "the best gift to man" must have greatly impressed Lila's young mind.

Chapter 7

High School Days

1. At High School

Eliza went to Galesburg High School for four years from 1867 till 1871. The first high school in the State of Illinois was founded in Chicago in 1856, and thereafter over a period of several years, 20 public high schools were built. The curriculum of the Chicago high schools consisted of Classics, English, and Teacher's courses. Eliza chose the English Course. For general subjects, she took History, Algebra, Geometry, Geography, Natural History (Animals, Plants, Minerals, Soil), Music, and as electives, Modern Foreign Language, Mathematics and Surveying .

Almost all the teachers at Eliza's high school were also professors at Knox College. Eliza was a bright student. She was interested in many things, and was curious and enthusiastic. At the time Eliza was a high school student, most entered the school in order to gain qualification to enter college. Eliza after graduating from high school had a wish to enter Knox College as her sister and brother had done. From the second floor of her home, she dreamed of studying specialized subjects at the college in the main building with the pointed tower. She was interested in studying Humanities, but wondered which specific field she would like to study. She thought about her long term goals and, probably thought of her future career.

2. Reading *Uncle Tom's Cabin*

Soon after entering high school, Eliza became a Sunday School teacher. Pastors of the church saw in her the ability to be a Bible teacher and therefore asked her to teach Sunday School. Perhaps the directors of the Sunday School may have asked her as well. Maybe even Cordelia, her mother with devout faith, encouraged her to become a Sunday School teacher. Every Sunday morning, Eliza told stories from Bible and other sources. In one of the stories, there was an account of Mrs. Stowe, the daughter of Preacher Lyman Beecher of the Religious Reconstruction Movement.

One of the main characters in the book was Uncle Tom, a black slave with strong beliefs, but the plot was that of one family escaping. The story can be summarized as follows. Plantation owner Mr. Shelby in Kentucky had to sell his slaves due to his debts, and a black slave Tom, Harry and his mother Eliza, and her husband George were to be sold to another plantation owner. Finding themselves in a difficult situation George and Eliza decided to escape to Canada, and run away under cover of darkness. On the way, Eliza held her children in her arms crossing over the frozen Ohio river ready to die if necessary. However they were helped by Quakers in Indiana. George was separated from his wife and children but fortunately reunited finally reaching their goal of getting to Canada.

The scene is described as such:

> George and his wife stood arm in arm, as the boat neared the small town of Amherstberg, in Canada. His breath grew thick and short; a mist gathered before his eyes; he silently pressed the little hand that lay trembling on his arm. The bell rang; the boat stopped. Scarcely seeing what he did, he looked out his baggage, and gathered his little party. The little company were landed on the shore. They stood still till the boat had cleared; and then, with tears and embracings, the husband and wife, with their wondering child in their arms, knelt down and lifted up their hearts to God!

'T was something like the burst from death to life;
From the grave's cerements to the robes of heaven;
From sin's dominion, and from passion's strife,
To the pure freedom of a soul forgiven;
Where all the bonds of death and hell are riven,
And mortal puts on immortality,
When Mercy's hand hath turned the golden key,
And Mercy's voice hath said, *Rejoice, thy soul is free.*"

The little party were soon guided, by Mrs. Smyth, to the hospitable abode of a good missionary, whom Christian charity has placed here as a shepherd to the out-cast and wandering, who are constantly finding an asylum on this shore.
Who can speak the blessedness of that first day of freedom? . . . . They had nothing more than the birds of the air, or the flowers of the field,—yet they could not sleep for joy. "O, ye who take freedom from man, with what words shall ye answer it to God?" [1]

This part is from Chapter 37 and the book consists of 45 chapters, and the subtitle of this chapter is "Freedom". When Eliza read this part and talked to the children, she again thought of the meaning of the situation and the content concerning freedom from slavery.

3. Galesburg and the "Underground Railroad"

One of the causes of the Civil War was slavery. The characters appearing in the novel *Uncle Tom's Cabin* were in fact representatives of slaves. In the Southern States in 1790, there were a little less than 700,000 slaves. But the figure increased threefold in 1830 and kept on growing. By 1860 the slave population had increased to four million people.

Whites owning plantations in the South produced cotton, which was in those days were called "White Gold." They sold it and with this income paid for food and industrial products. In order to gain a profit they bought slaves from Africa, who were inexpensive laborers, and forced them to work in terrible conditions.

> The slave is a human being, divested [stripped] of all rights—reduced to the level of a brute—a mere 'chattel'.... In law, the slave has no wife, no children, no country, and no home. He can own nothing, possess nothing, acquire nothing, but what must belong to another. [2]

Obviously, among slaves, there were certain people who hoped to run away. Most of the slaves who wished to escape were males under 30 years old. There were slaves a lot older who wished to escape, but they had been caught and had been whipped, put into prison, and chained, or put in fetters, finally ending up half alive and half dead.

There were Christians who lived near the cotton plantations who wanted to help these slaves who wanted to escape. They secretly planned to help the desperate slaves flee to Canada. One of the methods to transfer the slaves was the establishment of an organization called the "Underground Railroad." This was an attempt to use the railroad and other means to smuggle slaves into Canada from station to station, city to city unseen by those trying to catch them. Members constituting the organization who helped slaves escape were Christians of various denominations as well as students of Oberlin College. This movement did not cover a wide area, but Galesburg where Eliza lived, happened to be one of the crucial points. Eliza was astonished when she heard that some of the members of the Galesburg First Presbyterian Church were involved in the "Underground Railroad" movement, and probably respected the brave action of these members.

Chapter 8
Confession of Faith

1. Questions on slavery

The date and month are not exactly certain, but most probably in 1868 just before becoming a Sunday School teacher, Eliza became a member of the Galesburg First Presbyterian Church and as such would be able to receive Holy Communion. By making a "Confession of Faith," Eliza confessed her faith in the Gospel of Jesus Christ. Eliza was probably advised by the pastor of Church to make her "Confession of Faith." She may have consulted with her mother Cordelia. And her mother gave her strong support.

Eliza had expressed her intention and gave her strong support to confess her faith. However, she would have several lingering doubts. One of her doubts was about on slavery. Eliza was growing as an idealistic but sympathetic girl. Her doubt was why slavery existed, and how slaves could be liberated from such conditions.

2. Liberation from sin

The pastor's explanation was provocative: "Slavery, though people are slaves of sin is the sign of expression of acting freedom given by God. Slavery must be reformed or abolished, but all the people in the name of God should be "liberated from sin," and become real "free men." The pastor said that this was true and suggested several sections in Bible and read them.

In the Gospel according to John, it reads as follows:

> Jesus then said to the Jews who had believed in him, "If you con-
> tinue in my word, you are truly my disciples, and you will know the
> truth, and the truth will make you free." They answered him, "We
> are descendants of Abraham, and have never been in bondage to any
> one. How is it that you say, 'You will be made free'?"
> Jesus answered them, "Truly, truly, I say to you, every one who
> commits sin is a slave to sin. The slave does not continue in the
> house for ever; the son continues for ever. So if the Son makes you
> free, you will be free indeed. (John 8:31-36)

In Eliza's time, there was a shelf of annotations of the Bible at
Sunday School, and among them was "Barnes' Annotation." Albert
Barnes (1798-1870) was the pastor of the Philadelphia First Presbyterian Church, and had taught at Union Theological Seminary, and
his enormous annotations have provided a great contribution to the
study of the Bible. Barnes' Annotation explains as follows:

> 'The Truth shall make you free.' The truth here means the Christian
> religion. Compare Gal. iii. 1; Col. i. 6. The doctrines of the true reli-
> gion shall make you free. The condition of a sinner is that of a cap-
> tive or a slave to sin. He is one who serves and obeys the dictates of
> an evil heart, and the corrupt desires of an evil nature, Rom. vi. 16,
> 17, 19, 20; vii. 6, 8, 11; viii.21; Acts viii.23; Gal. iv. 3, 9. The effect
> of the gospel is to break this hard bondage to sin, and to set the sin-
> ner free. The service of God is freedom from degrading vices and
> carnal propensities; from the slavery of passion and inordinate de-
> sires; and a cheerful and delightful surrender of ourselves to Him
> whose yoke is easy, and whose burden is light. [1]

By "God saving us" we the sinners will be freed from "the slavery
of sin" and will wholeheartedly obey God, and be able to serve others. If Eliza had read this Annotation, she would have touched on the
truth of the Gospel.

3. Confession of faith

Moreover, Eliza had probably read John Calvin's "Handbook for Faith" and "Catechism of the Church of Geneva" which the pastor had recommended. (Calvin's main work is "The Institute of Christian Religion," (1536-59), but the "Handbook of Faith" (1536) is an abridged form of "The Institute of Christian Religion" for beginners, and the "Catechism of the Church of Geneva" is an extract of "The Institute of Christian Religion.")

The Bible has often witnessed that mankind is a slave of sin. What the Bible says is that since mankind's spirit has become far apart from God's righteousness, mankind's thoughts and desires and wishes can become vulgar, wicked, illegal and disgraced. This means that the mind is completely affected by the poison of sin, and at the same time cannot bear the fruit of sin. So mankind commits sin in the unexpected urgent situation. The reason why people commit sin is that they will agree to admit committing sin light heartedly and favorably. Due to the corruptness of desire, man indeed hates all the righteousness of God, and can become enthusiastic about all kinds of evil behavior. So it is said that man does not have free will to decide good or evil.[2]

Man, in his nature cannot see due to decadence and the corruption of feelings. People are not able to have real understanding, and admit to not being able to get involved in good deeds. Man has the potential to be given up by God and abandoned as he is, but he will stay ignorant and immersed in a lawless state. Thus, man in order to know God's salvation rightfully should be shown by God, corrected in God's love, and reformed to obey God's righteousness.[3]

All the glory and praise must be in the hand of God. In order to retain real peace and rest in conscience, we have to understand and confess that all the blessings derive from God. This blessing without consideration comes from only God's affection and compassion, even our own values and the effects of our deeds. . . . [4]

In the spring of 1868, just before becoming a Sunday School

teacher, Eliza Winn confessed to the "Gospel of Jesus Christ" at a service of the Galesburg First Presbyterian Church.

Chapter 9

Meeting with Thomas Winn

1. Graduating from College and studying for an extra year

Eliza entered Knox College in 1870, and graduated in 1874, studying for four years. But she stayed at the college and studied for one more year. She was a Liberal Art student and chose English Course. After entering college over the first two to three years, she studied History, Algebra, Geometry, Geography, Natural History (Zoology and Botany), Music, Old Testament, New Testament, and Christian Ethics as required subjects. In her third and fourth year, she took English Studies, Phonetics, Composition, Vocabularies, History of the English Language as specialized subjects. She also took French as her Modern Foreign Language. It is not known whether Eliza had actually written her graduation thesis.

Eliza was interested in many fields and was studious. She was a serious student and was rated at the top of her class in most of the subjects she took. After completing four years of studies, Eliza graduated from Knox College. But unlike other students in general, she stayed one more year at the College and studied Medical and Nursing Studies. Concerning medical studies, she learned clinical medicine covering diagnosis treatment and instruction and health care of prognosis of the injured. And regarding "Nursing", she learned the treatment of sickness, help in healthcare, protection of illness and advice, and education and instruction. Eliza took these courses as an auditing student.

The reason Eliza as a student of Liberal Arts went on to study science courses is evident. Before graduation, she had decided on her career. In order to accomplish her goal she needed to study clinical medicine and knowledge and technical skills of nursing. Trained in the Liberal Arts as well as medicine, Eliza was to eventually establish her future career in the context of the wife of Thomas Winn and the propagation of Christianity.

2. Family background of Thomas Winn

Thomas Clay Winn was born as the third son of Presbyterian pastor John Winn and his wife Mary Winn on June 29, 1851 at Flemington, Liberty County, Georgia. He had two brothers and later on a sister and a brother were born.

Flemington is a small town located east of Hinseville, with population at that time of a little over 100. Hinseville had a population of 1500. People living in the area were mostly involved in farming and forestry, and partly in dairy farming. Though the land was not fertile, the farmland as well as the forest of the Appalachian Mountains extended to this area and prairie fields existed here and there.

The name Hinseville" derives from "Town of Hinehas." Hinehas, a great bishop was the son of Moses' brother Aron. The people of Israel under Hinehas had stopped Bal Peor, the religion worshipped by Moab, and stopped the women of Moab and Midean from having intercourse with the people of Israel. In this way Hinehas saved the integrity of Jahawe worship. (Numbers 25:6-15) This is how the name Hinesville originated.

Thomas' father was the pastor of the Presbyterian Church in this small town of Hinesville. People who lived in this town and its vicinity originally immigrated in the 17th century and were Scotch Irish. An account on Scotch Irish is given by Mary B. Norton et. al: *A People and a Nation* as follows:

The largest group of white non-English immigrants to America was the Scotch-Irish, chiefly descended from Presbyterian Scots who had settled in Protestant portions of Ireland during the seventeenth century. Perhaps as many as 250,000 Scotch-Irish people moved to the colonies. Fleeing economic distress and religious discrimination at home — Irish law favored Anglicans over Presbyterians and other dissenters — they were lured as well by hopes of obtaining land in America. Like the Germans, the Scotch-Irish often landed in Philadelphia. They also moved west and south from that city, settling chiefly in the western portions of Pennsylvania, Maryland, Virginia, and the Carolinas. Frequently unable to afford to buy any acreage, they squatted on land belonging to Indian tribes, land speculators, or colonial governments. [1]

3. Parents of Thomas Winn

Not much information is available today concerning the background of Thomas' father and mother. However, according to *Nihon no Shito: Thomas C. Winn Den* (Disciple of Japan, The Life of Thomas C. Winn), 4th Edition, both were no doubt people with strong religious beliefs and charitable thoughts.

Thomas' father as a pastor of the Presbyterian Church spoke of the wonder of God, and led the service of Holy Communion. The mother took care of the family and raised five children, served the church, and was a devout Christian. There was a common worry for Thomas' parents. Thomas had been physically weak since he was born, and experienced occasional stomachaches. It could be that Thomas suffered from chronic gastritis. So he was taking medicine prescribed by the doctor and was on a restricted diet.

The income of Thomas' father as a pastor of the town's church was considerably low. So Thomas' brothers went to a nearby ranch and worked part time. Thomas went along with his brothers and watched how cows were raised, milked, and dairy products processed. He most likely helped with dairy farming.

4. Winn's family moves to Galesburg, Illinois

In 1858, when Thomas was seven years old, the Winns decided to move to Illinois. Rev. Winn somehow got to know George Gale, the founder of Knox College. Due to his request, John Winn got the position of teaching subjects related to Christianity.[2]

The Winns moved to Galesburg. They lived in a small house at the outskirts of the town. (The Winns did not move again until 1897, and their address was 501 East Losey Street, Galesburg.) Soon after they moved to Galesburg, Thomas' mother went to New York. She had to say farewell to Samuel Brown, her brother. Samuel Robbins Brown (1810-80) was the older brother of Thomas' mother and thus was an uncle to Thomas. This time, Samuel Brown was to be leaving as the first missionary dispatched to Japan by the Dutch Reformed Church of the U.S.A. When Thomas' mother Mary came back from New York, she brought with her an elderly woman, Phoebe Brown. This woman happened to be the grandmother of Thomas, and she lived with his mother's sister (Thomas' aunt) right next to Thomas' home. For this reason, the town of Galesburg happened to welcome the Winns and the Browns at the same time.

Chapter 10

Love, Career, and Thomas' Call

1. Love and decision of future career

Eliza first met Thomas was when the Winns moved to Galesburg. Eliza, or Lila, was 5 years old, and Thomas was 7 years old. They probably met as children at Sunday School and later at the elementary school. Lila had one brother and two sisters. Thomas would have been friends with Lila's brother. It is not known, but Thomas and Lila would also have been teachers at the Sunday School about the same time. The situation for them to get to know each other was set, but for 10 years they were not aware of each other.

It is hard to imagine when Eliza came to consider Thomas her "boy friend" or Thomas becoming aware of Eliza as his "girl friend," and how they eventually became intimate and talk frankly on any topic with each other.

It was later on in 1871, that relationship progressed. Eliza was a freshman at Knox College. Thomas was then in his Junior year. However in 1872, Thomas left Knox College, transferring to Amherst College. He had decided to become a pastor. What was then his motive in making a drastic change? It was partly that his relationship with Eliza became closer, and Thomas felt a calling to become a missionary. The author suspects that the career of missionary and Thomas' wife propagating the Gospel in a foreign land was becoming more realistic in her mind.

2. Phoebe Brown's religious faith

Thomas did not speak to anyone of his call to become a missionary. However, when Thomas and Eliza talked about their future, he explained that his call for missionary work had been influenced by his grandmother Phoebe Brown. Soon after his grandmother's move to Galesburg, he was able to meet with her frequently. In fact they lived right next door so these meetings were easily arranged.

When Phoebe Hinsdale Brown moved next to Thomas' home, she was 75 years old but quite vigorous. She was kind to her grandson and probably shared her years of wisdom and experience with him. When their conversations turned to Thomas' health, she said, "Having a weak body means that God will surely make it strong and healthy. It is written in the Bible." It is quite likely that Thomas would not have fully understood what his grandmother was saying.

Phoebe shared her own life experiences with her young grandson, Thomas. She was born in the countryside in New York State, losing her parents when still young. She had a tough time, but went to a Congregational Church and was strengthened in her belief. When she was 23, she married a house painter named Brown. They lived poorly but purely, and although still poor gave an offering to the church from their limited income. The words of the Bible and words of the sermon at the church services often moved her heart. She started writing but could not buy pen and ink, so made a pen from a bird feather, and made ink out of tree barks. She studied on her own and wrote an annotation to the "Song of Solomon" in the Old Testament. She wrote a lot of hymns, but still wrote poems on an overwhelming number of topics.

Thomas had heard the process of how her most famous hymn "I love to steal awhile away" was written.

I love to steal awhile away
From every cumbering care,
And spend the hours of closing day

In humble, grateful prayer [1]

When Phoebe wrote this hymn, she had four children and a sister who was ill and was very busy with housework. Every evening, however, she made it a custom to pray in the back orchard of the next door neighbor's huge house. One time, the neighbor's wife suspected that Phoebe has entered her orchard to steal fruit. Phoebe was so upset that she was suspected of stealing fruit, that she lost her ability to speak and just left. And that night when everybody had gone to sleep, she expressed her feeling about this situation in a poem and sent it to the neighbor. [2]

Three years after Grandma Phoebe came to Galesburg, she was called home to heaven. She was 78 years old. Poor Thomas, he could not hear "stories" anymore from his grandmother. The funeral took place at the Galesburg First Presbyterian Church, and the small chapel was filled. Thomas was there with his mother and the assembled mourners all sang her now familiar hymn, "I Love to Steal Awhile Away."

3. The Influence of Uncle Samuel Brown

When Thomas told Eliza about his call to become a missionary, he told her that uncle Samuel Brown was another person who greatly influenced him. In the winter of 1868, when Thomas was 17, he was most likely taken by some member of his family from Georgia to New York, travelling on a train over tracks just laid. The purpose of the trip was to have a medical check-up of his illness and receive treatment. The following account is the answer to the question of what was his most thankful moment asked by a guest at the missionary residence hall in Kanazawa when Rev. Winn was quite old in 1931.

When I was seventeen and going on eighteen, I stayed at the house of my uncle, Dr. Samuel R. Brown. He had just returned from Japan to begin a two-year furlough in the United States at the direction of the Board of Foreign Missions of the Dutch Reformed Church (U.S.A.). I stayed at his residence through the winter of 1868. The illness I had suffered from became more pronounced, and I felt acute pain day and night. I could not even sleep. The doctor prescribed medicine, but it was not a great help. My uncle and his wife treated me very well, but I somehow felt lonely---- I prayed to God about my illness. I made an oath to God, and promised that if I were healed, I would go anywhere that God sent me. I was very sick for two weeks, but then, miraculously, I recovered. I was very happy— I became physically strong after that, and I could study and play sports like other youngsters— I eventually made my way to Japan toward the end of the year 1877. [3]

Uncle Samuel must have told a lot of stories to Thomas at his New York home. He told Thomas about Christian missions, the work of the missionary, about Far Eastern countries, the religious situation in China and Japan, the translation of the Bible, and the difficulty speaking in Chinese or Japanese. Uncle Samuel's talk led young Thomas straight to the calling for missionary work later in his life.

Staying at his uncle's home in New York, he recovered from his illness. Eliza would later listen intensely to Thomas talking with his bright eyes on mission to China and Japan.

4. Mary Winn, Thomas' mother's advice

There was one other thing that Thomas told Eliza which concerned him becoming a missionary. It was what his mother said that was entirely unexpected.

Thomas was the third child born to John and Mary. When completing his second year at Knox College, Thomas received a letter from his oldest brother Henry, who was practicing dentistry in Hong Kong. Henry said that Thomas should quit college and study at the Dentistry School, with his tuition covered by his brother. Eventually they would work together as dentists in Hong Kong and their future success would be secured.

Thomas was tempted to follow his brother's offer, and reported to his mother that "I hope to accept my brother's kind offer." However, his mother was not happy with this development and replied," Why don't you become a preacher?" Thomas' mother Mary had a strong Christian faith. She was ready to let her son serve God when his health improved.

Thomas did not expect this development. Thomas no doubt shared all this with Eliza.

Chapter 11

Becoming a Missionary and Getting Married

1. Eliza's call and decision

Eliza had probably discussed with her mother Cordelia the essence of her talk with Thomas. Good communication between mother and daughter had already been established, but Cordelia knew well that Eliza was now at a critical turning point in her life. To become the wife of a missionary to a foreign land meant that she would also be a missionary herself. Would Eliza be able to endure this great task? On the other hand, Eliza and Thomas had become close and the calling and their affectionate relation both came from God. Listening to Eliza's talk about her future, Cordelia finally spoke. "The way you are going, decide by yourself. Pray to God and listen whether you are going on the right path." Eliza prayed to God as her mother had said, and Eliza finally confirmed her wish.

Eliza said something to Thomas like, "I have decided. Just as your mother had told me, 'why don't you become a Preacher.' I will be the wife of a Preacher."

By the time Eliza made her decision, she had graduated from College, and remained there to study "Clinical Medicine" and "Nursing." She was aware that in her role as a missionary she would need this knowledge and skill.

For those who knew her, however, Eliza's decision was perhaps a

surprise. Most people thought Eliza naturally would choose an "easier life" and some thought that it was still not too late. Eliza's family was quite wealthy, and being intelligent and good natured, it was
hard to understand why she would choose a life of poverty and difficulty. Some people might have made suggestions to her along these
lines. However, Eliza knew her situation very well. Her decision
would not be changed. It was a decision based on her faith.

2. Thomas and Eliza become missionaries

Thomas left Knox College in 1871, entered Divinity School, and
decided to become a pastor. In 1872, he transferred to Amherst College in Massachusetts, and graduated in 1873. After that, he studied
at McCormick Theological Seminary for one year, and worked as
temporary pastor at Farmer City, Illinois for another year. He then
went on and studied for 2 years at Union Theological Seminary in
New York, graduating there in the spring of 1877. In May that same
year, Thomas was assigned as a missionary from the Board of Foreign Missions of the Presbyterian Church (North) in the United
States. On this occasion, Dr. Lowrie (John C.), Director of Foreign
Mission Board addressed words to Thomas, and what he said is as
follows:

> The Board of Foreign Missions had at this time assigned a young
> man to stay in Yokohama, Japan and work there. The name of the
> person is George W. Knox. He would be practicing as medical doc-
> tor and also get involved in missionary work, and help Dr. Hepburn
> who was translating the Bible into Japanese. Thus Thomas Winn
> had to be assigned to a remote area in Japan. [1]

In the summer of 1877, Thomas preached at the Presbyterian
Church of Mount Carmel in Southern Illinois, and on September 19th,
was ordained into the Gospel ministry of the Oneida Presbyterian
Church, located 30 kilometers northeast of Galesburg.

Eliza on her part had also applied to the Board of Foreign Mis-

Double Wedding
From left: Eliza Caroline Willard, Thomas Clay Winn,
Joseph Joachim Lampe, Emma Almira Willard (Eliza's elder sister)

sions of the Presbyterian Church in the United States (North) and to the Woman's Presbyterian Board of Missions of the Northwest and was accepted. The Woman's Presbyterian Board of Missions in Chicago would assign and guarantee to pay the cost of her missionary activities. Also the Board of Foreign Missions of the Presbyterian Church had formally assigned her as an "associate missionary," meaning the wife of a missionary. (In Japan, the category "woman missionary" is often used.)

3. Wedding of Eliza and Thomas and the farewell party

On September 20, 1877, Elisa and Thomas were married at the Galesburg First Presbyterian Church. The wedding was simple, but the couple was blessed by God and those who attended. On Eliza's side of the family, those who attended were her mother Cordelia, her brother, and her sisters, as well as friends of Lila. [She and her one sister were married in a double ceremony.]

On Thomas' side, his parents, John and Mary Winn, brothers and sisters, Thomas' aunt and friend and acquaintances attended the wedding.

Two months later, on November 18, after the Sunday service at church, a farewell party for Eliza and Thomas was held. Members of the church wished them best luck on their journeys, and prayed for God's protection and guidance toward their endeavor. But the congregation of the church felt sad that they would no longer be able to attend the service with them and chat after the service anymore.

There were gifts presented by the elders of the Church. What Thomas received is not known, but Eliza was presented with several pieces of clothing for female missionaries. The church sending out any missionary abroad consulted with the Foreign Mission Board to help them prepare for their journey. It was a custom that the sending church presented missionary clothes as a farewell gift.

On Saturday November 24, Eliza and Thomas left the town of Galesburg. They had no idea that they would end up in Kanazawa, Japan.

"By faith Abraham obeyed when he was called to go out to a place which he was to receive as an inheritance; and he went out, not knowing where he was to go." (Hebrew 11:8)

Chapter 12

Arriving in Japan and the Assigned Site

1. Three missionary couples reaching Yokohama

On December 26, 1877, the Pacific Liner "City of Peking" carrying Eliza and Thomas Winn reached the Port of Yokohama. It took the couple 32 days to reach Yokohama after leaving Galesburg.

The route of their journey was as follows: Eliza and Thomas boarded the Kansas Pacific Railroad train from Galesburg to Cheyenne, and there transferred to the Pacific Railroad and reached San Francisco a few days later. They then boarded a ship to Japan and finally reached their destination.

The details of their journey are not recorded, but there were two other missionary couples assigned by the Board of Foreign Missions of the Presbyterian Church (North) in the United States who were on the same ship, and Eliza and Thomas probably were comfortable talking to them. The two couples were George W. Knox and Thomas T. Alexander and their wives.

George William Knox (1853-1912) was a Presbyterian missionary who graduated from Hamilton College and the Oberlin School of Theology. After he arrived in Japan, he taught at the Hepburn School founded by Mrs. Hepburn, and at Tokyo Union Seminary. The Seminary later became Meiji Gakuin University, where George Knox taught Systematic Theology and Biblical Studies.

Thomas Theron Alexander (1850-1902) was Thomas Winn's best

friend. He was born the son of a farmer at Mount Horof in Tennessee. Graduating from Maryville College, he became an assistant for 2 years and subsequently later entered Union Theological Seminary. After graduation, he went to Japan with Thomas and later taught at Tsukiji College (founded privately by Presbyterian Missionary Christopher Carrothers.)

After a while, he taught English at Tokyo Union Eiwa School, but later due to the expanding activities of the Presbyterian Church was involved in mission work in the Kansai area, and established the Osaka Kita Church, Osaka Minami Church, Nihon Kirisuto Kyoto Church, and the Icchi Girls' School. In 1894, he was invited to be a Professor at Meiji Gakuin Theological School, taking the position vacated by George Knox, and devoted his time to the education of Divinity students.

Thomas Alexander was a classmate of Thomas Winn at Union Theological School. They were good friends and continued a good relationship throughout their lives. He made the decision to come to Japan because Thomas Winn told him about his decision, and persuaded him to go with him. While working as a missionary in the Kansai, as his area included the Hokuriku district, Thomas Alexander extended his support and understanding toward the Winn's activities in Kanazawa. It was due to Alexander's request that the Winns came to two churches in Osaka to help him.

2. Staying at Samuel Brown's house

After landing in Yokohama, the Winns stayed at the home of Thomas' uncle Samuel Brown for several days. Samuel Brown was occupied in translating the Bible, teaching and preaching, but quite a few of his relatives stayed at his house on business or in mission. So with these other relatives, the Winns were welcomed. This opportunity with other missionaries was a special experience that they could not have dreamed to be possible.

The group staying at Samuel Brown's house included: Dr. Brown

Samuel R. Brown
(Copyright of photo: Yokohama Archives of History)

and his wife, their eldest daughter Julia Maria along with her husband Mr.Lowder [British Consul], their two daughters Hattie and
Louise, and their oldest son Robert Brown and his wife. Also staying with them were Thomas' older brother Henry, his wife and their
children Majorie and Fret, and Thomas and Eliza Winn. This group
amounted to 14 people all together. [1]

After that, for two years until September 1879, Thomas and Eliza
lived at a small house in Yamate in Yokohama. Their goals during
this particular period of time was carefully planned.
(1) To get in touch with Dr. James Hepburn who was in charge of
   Christian Mission in Japan.
(2) To study the Japanese language.
(3) To assist the English School in both Tokyo and Yokohama.
(4) To become prepared to get involved in missionary work after two
   years.

3. Dr. Samuel Brown's background

Eliza, staying at Dr. Samuel Brown's house was impressed with Dr. Brown as a person. His abundant knowledge and his enormous work in translating the Bible into Japanese was just astonishing. She would have heard of Dr. Brown's background from Thomas.

Samuel Robbins Brown (1810-1880) was a missionary dispatched by the Dutch Reformed Church in the United States. He was born in East Windsor, Connecticut, and went on to study at Yale College, and Columbia Theological School, eventually graduated from Union Theological Seminary. In 1838, Samuel Brown went to China and became the head of the Morrison Academy established to educate Chinese students. In 1847, he returned to United States because of his wife's illness and became head of the Rome Academy in New York, but was called to pastor at Sand Beach Church in 1851. (Miss Kidder, the founder of Ferris Girls' School happened to be a member of this Church.)

Following his work in New York, in 1859 he went to Japan as a missionary. He lived in Jobutsu-ji (temple) in Kanagawa. This was after he was awarded Ph. D. in Theology from New York State University. In 1869, he along with Miss Kidder became teachers at Niigata English School, but the school could not pay his salary and so he resigned in one year, returned to Yokohama and started to teach at the Yokohama Shubunkan School. In 1872, he was nominated as a chair of the Committee of Translating the New Testament, and worked with Dr. Hepburn, D. C. Green and Masatsuna Okuno. This translation resulted in the publication of the *Shinyaku Zensho* (Complete Version of New Testament), in 1880. Brown's School was founded in 1873 at Yamate, Yokohama and he taught English and Theology and educated young students as the "Yokohama Band", including Masahisa Uemura, Youichi Honda and Kajinosuke Ibuka.

Miss Kidder as mentioned before is Mary Eddy Kidder (1834-1910). After coming back from Niigata to Yokohama, she taught at Hepburn's School which was started by Mrs. Hepburn, but later de-

Dr. James Curtis Hepburn
(Copyright of photo: Yokohama Archives of History)

veloped into "Ferris Waei Gakko" (Ferris Girls' School.) [The school was named after Isaac Ferris (1798-1873) and his son John Mason Ferris (1825-1911) who both acted as directors of Foreign Mission Board of Dutch Reformed Church in the United States.] She got married to Rev. Edward Miller in 1873. She was primarily a missionary in Tokyo, but also in Ueda, Kochi, Morioka, and other areas in Japan.

4. Meeting Dr. Hepburn

A few days after arriving Yokohama, three missionary couples visited the clinic of Dr. Hepburn in the Yokohama Foreign Settlement, greeted him and were notified of the future schedules. Dr. Hepburn had been a missionary for many years and had been asked to provide direction to the missionary group assigned to Japan by the Board of Foreign Missions of the Presbyterian Church (North) in United States. Eliza had heard about Dr. Hepburn from Thomas and knew something about him. This meeting with Dr. Hepburn had a great influence on their faith and on the mission work of Eliza and Thomas.

James Curtis Hepburn (1815-1911) was born in Milton, Pennsylvania. He studied Chemistry at Princeton University and specialized in Ophthalmology at the University of Pennsylvania. He earned a Ph. D. in Medicine, and went to China as a medical missionary in 1841. He was involved in mission and medical practice in China, but returned to United States due to the illness of his wife Clara. Back in the United States, he practiced as an eye doctor and did well. In 1859, hearing that Japan had opened its doors, Dr. Hepburn went to Japan and started a clinic, first at Jobutsu-ji (temple) in Kanagawa, and then at the Yokohama Foreign Settlement. In all he treated several hundred thousand Japanese patients. This was despite the fact that at that time, foreigners were being murdered in Kanagawa due to anti-foreign sentiments, with fifteen people killed in three years.) Besides his medical practice, Dr. Hepburn translated the Gospel into Japanese and also invented the "Hepburn Roman Style Alphabets" — a new method of transcribing the Japanese language. In 1863, he and his wife founded the Hepburn's School, and there introduced a new style of Girls' education. Also in 1874, the Yokohama Presbyterian Church (the present day Yokohama Shiro Church) was founded. [2] Dr. Hepburn was appointed as the chair of the Bible Translation Committee, and completely committed himself to this project along with Masahisa Uemura and Kajinosuke Ibuka. In 1888, the efforts resulted in the publication of the *Kyuyaku Zennsho* (Complete Old Testament). Then in 1889, Dr. Hepburn became the president of Meiji Gakuin University, a position he held until 1891. He was also co-editor with Hideteru Yamamoto of the *Seisho Jiten* (Dicitonary of the Bible). Thomas and Eliza made full use of this dictionary in their mission work.

5. Studying Japanese and getting to know Japanese culture and customs

Shortly after Thomas arrived in Japan, his old illness returned.

For half a year he had a gripping pain in the stomach. Eliza worried about her husband's health.

However, Eliza and Thomas continued their careful study of Japanese and daily conversation. At that time the popular Japanese textbook was Johann Joseph Hoffmann's *Nihon Bunten* (A Japanese Grammar, 1868), and Dr. Hepburn's *Kaiwa Nihongo* (Japanese Conversation, 1863). Since Dr. Hepburn was available, Eliza and Thomas could ask any question they might have regarding "Japanese Conversation".

In studying Japanese and daily conversation, individual instruction was given to them by a Japanese private teacher on a regular basis. Both studied quite hard, and so they improved greatly. They had also learned from the Japanese teacher a lot on Japanese culture. Going out, they tried to talk to Japanese people about Japanese religion, Japanese life style and how they see and think.

6. Thomas teaches at Ballagh's School

Thomas Winn started teaching at Ballagh's School in the early summer of 1878 in Yokohama. Eliza was pregnant then, and probably did not teach at this school.

The Ballagh's School was founded by James Ballagh and was originally called Takashima's School, and the English School. In the beginning Japanese students gathered together in a small hall and studied English and the Bible.

James Hamilton Ballagh (1832-1920) was from New York, and graduated from Rutgers College and New Brunswick Theological School. A missionary assigned by the Dutch Reformed Church in United States, he came to Japan in 1852. He lived in Yokohama, and coordinated his mission work with Dr. Brown and Dr. Hepburn, started the Yokohama English School in 1862 and Takashima's School in 1871 and taught English and the Bible. James Ballagh was a very intense person with a burning passion for Christian missions. He had always prayed before teaching his classes, and continued this custom in Japan. In 1865, he baptized Ryusan (Mototaka)Yano, his Japanese teacher, and this was the first person to be baptized by a Protestant missionary in Japan. When Yano asked Ballagh to baptize him, both Ballagh and Hepburn tried to convince him not to be baptized, as grave danger would likely fall over to him and his family. However Yano was determined and did not listen to their advice.

Eliza was pregnant but could not stay still, she wished to talk immediately about Christianity in Japanese, and so sometimes would go outside. She loved to talk with farmers near Negishi. [3]

7. Assigned to go to Kanazawa

While staying in Yokohama for two years, Thomas Winn along with several other people went on a trip to Niigata passing through Naoetsu, and observed the area and returned to Yokohama through Usui Pass. By coincidence he met with Shozo Hattori, the pastor of the Presbyterian Church in Shimonoseki, who then invited Rev. Winn to preach in the Shimonoseki area. Pastor Hattori contacted the Foreign Mission Board in Japan and submitted a request to assign Rev. Winn to Shimonoseki. As a result of his travels, Rev. Winn was asked by the Mission Board to provide a consultation.

There was also an inquiry addressed to Dr. Hepburn from the Ishikawa Prefectural Normal Junior High School which was looking for a teacher of both Science and English. It was the summer of 1879. Through Rev. Ballagh, Dr. Hepburn privately reached out to Thomas Winn as to whether or not he would preach in the Hokuriku district.

Thomas and Eliza prayed and listened to God's guidance, and both were involved in this discussion about the mission. Although Kanazawa was the largest city in Northern Japan, Western culture had been introduced more slowly than in other areas. It was an area of the country where the Buddhist influence was very strong, and therefore a difficult place to spread Christianity. But Rev. Winn was determined to work in such a challenging environment and he and

Eliza decided to commit themselves to the " Hokuriku Mission" [5]

8. Assignment to go to Kanazawa and Dr. Hepburn's advice

Trying to propagate Christianity in the Hokuriku district, located northwest of Tokyo had been a challenge for the Foreign Mission Board in Japan since 1869. In 1873, Japan removed the national ban on Christianity in response to European and American protests, so the situation had greatly changed. It was now possible to propagate Christian beliefs in cities other than in the former Foreign Settlements of Yokohama, Tokyo, Kobe, and Nagasaki.

In the summer of 1878, Dr. Hepburn brought together a meeting of the Foreign Mission Board in Japan and decided to send Rev. and Mrs. Winn along with Mary True, woman missionary teaching at Shin Sakae Girls' School, to the Hokuriku district.

Soon after the meeting at Dr. Hepburn's Clinic started, Dr. Hepburn announced Thomas and Eliza Winn's assignment to Kanazawa. Dr. Hepburn gave them the following advice. He had been a missionary to Japan for many years, and so made several valuable points.

(1) The job descriptions of the missionary and female missionary.
(2) Explanation of the Bible in the Japanese language.
(3) The cultural and religious situation of the assigned district.
(4) Financial assistance as well as transportation expenses back to the United States.

(1)The job description of the missionary and female missionary:
The main work of the missionary is to propagate the Gospel. So a theological understanding and research of the Gospels must always be continued, with the goal of trying to build a new church. Also, the missionary couple's conduct needed to be a model of behavior for the assigned district.

(2)Explanation of the Bible in the Japanese Language:
There are words in the Bible that cannot be explained correctly in Japanese. The meaning and idea should be told accurately, so it is

necessary to carefully prepare and try to explain by giving examples and using various ideas.

(3)On cultural and religious situations of the assigned district:

Kanazawa is located in a distant land, and culturally it is very conservative. It is said that Kanazawa is the "Kingdom of Buddhism", and so all must be well aware that the propagation of Christianity would be a difficult task. Guido Herman Fridolin Verbeck, a missionary of the Dutch Reformed Church in his record said that Rev. Winn and his family were assigned to Kanazawa, but that the region they were assigned to was so remote from other missionaries, that it was clear to everyone that they would face the same persecution as the early missionaries.[6]

(4)Financial Assistance and transportation expenses back to the United States:

The living expenses of missionaries was to be guaranteed but that they should be careful in not having problems of clothing, food, and living conditions with members of the church or with neighboring residents. Also considerable care handling of money between the Foreign Mission Board and the churches must be taken. Expenses covering furlough and transportation fees must be paid accordingly.

Dr. Hepburn was bald in front with white hair, and his age was 64 or 65. He was intelligent and thoughtful, and had a dignified appearance as the representative of the Foreign Mission Board in Japan. Thomas and Eliza had listened intently to his valuable advice. At that time Thomas had established with Dr. Hepburn the strong tie of master and disciple. In the *Letters of Thomas Winn*, there are often references to Dr. Hepburn's nephew.

Chapter 13

Arriving at Kanazawa and Starting to Preach

1. The ends of the earth

Thomas and Eliza Winn and several others left Yokohama for Kanazawa on September 23, 1879. The group included the Winns, their one year old baby Mary, and Mrs. True and her eleven year old daughter Annie. Accompanying them was the preacher from Tsuruga, Seikichi Hayashi, as well as a woman preacher, Sei Deguchi. Also in their group was the head of the Ishikawa Prefectural Normal Junior High School, Goro Numata, who was to be their guide.

And so they began their extremely arduous journey to Kanazawa. They traveled from Yokohama to Kobe by ship, then boarded a train from Kobe to Otani, Kyoto. From Otani they traveled to Otsu by rickshaw. The last leg of the journey was across Lake Biwa in a small steamboat, from Otsu to Shiotsu (the present day Nishi Asai). The journey from Yokohama to Otsu had gone well, but two hours before arriving at their final destination, Shiotsu, they met with a sudden storm. The little steamboat was like a leaf floating on the surface of the high waves. The entire journey took a total of five days.

The group finally arrived at Shiotsu late in the evening, around 10:00 pm. The innkeeper in Shiotsu looked at the group standing in the pouring rain, and refused to allow them in. He had never seen foreigners before. Their guide, Mr. Numata, looked all over town,

Route Winn's group took from Yokohama to Kanazawa
September 23~October 4, 1879

9 people travelled, taking 12 days.
Sept. 23: Left Yokohama by ship
Sept. 24: Arrive Kobe, stayed with
      O.H. Gulick
      Sept. 26: Rode train to Kyoto, met
      Jo Niijima of Doshisha. Train
      from Kyoto to Otani, rickshaw
      to Otsu. Crossed Lake Biwa by
      steam boat. Arrive Shiotsu.
      To Tsuruga by paranquin
Sept. 29: One group walked to Kanazawa,
      Winns rode ship to Kanaiwa
      But meets storm
Oct. 3:   Those who walked arrive
      Kanazawa. Went to
      Kanaiwa to meet Winns
Oct. 4:   Arrive Kanazawa by
      rickshaw

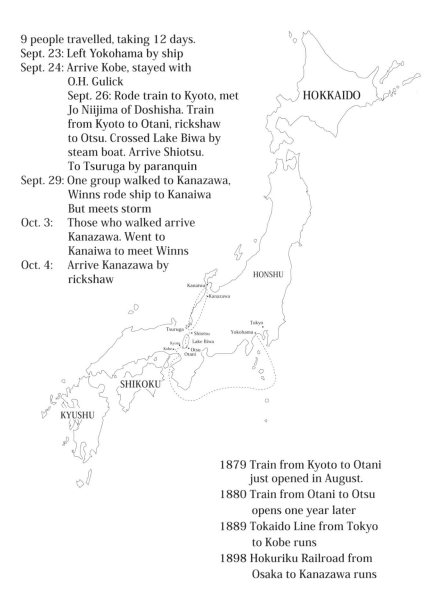

1879 Train from Kyoto to Otani
      just opened in August.
1880 Train from Otani to Otsu
      opens one year later
1889 Tokaido Line from Tokyo
      to Kobe runs
1898 Hokuriku Railroad from
      Osaka to Kanazawa runs

trying to find a place for them to stay, but was unsuccessful. He was at a loss as to what to do, and so finally went to a police station to ask for help. The policeman was able to persuade an innkeeper at an old inn to allow the group to stay there. They could finally eat supper, and stay at an inn.

Thomas and the group awoke the next morning to continue their journey. Thomas rode a rickshaw, and occasionally walked, and Eliza and the baby rode a palanquin. The group continued their strenuous trip, but finally arrived exhausted at Tsuruga on the Japan Sea. They had yet to reach their final destination, Kanazawa. There was not yet a railroad to Kanazawa, so they had to take a boat from Tsuruga to Kanazawa, before they would board yet another rickshaw, the final leg of their journey. Thomas murmured to Eliza, "Is this the end of the earth?"

This episode was recounted later by Eliza because it was so unusual, coming from Thomas. She knew that they had not come from deep desperation. The reference to the end of the earth comes from Isaiah 49:6, and is also conveyed in the sermon by Paul and Barnabas in the sermon at Antioch. The Lord says: "I will give you as a light to the nations, that my salvation may reach the end of the earth."

2. Arrival at Kanazawa after surviving a typhoon.

The following day they boarded another ship to complete their journey to Kanazawa. Shortly after leaving port they encountered a severe typhoon. The sea was terrifying to all on board. All luggage, including that of the Winns, was lost overboard. The items lost overboard included their bibles for preaching, religious tracts that they planned to distribute, provisions, clothing, and even memorabilia from their wedding. Passengers paled in fear, and children were crying. The ship drifted for hours in the strong winds. It was only through the skill of the experienced captain that they finally escaped danger. The next evening the ship finally weighed anchor, five miles from their final destination, the port of Kanaiwa. The wind continued to be strong, and the rain still came down hard, so that a barge could not be used to complete the journey. The tired passengers had to remain on the ship, and could not go ashore.

The next day, the boat continued on to the port of Kanaiwa, and the passengers were able to disembark. From this port they took a 3 hour rickshaw ride to where they would stay in Kanazawa. It had taken them 12 days from the time they left Yokohama for them to arrive finally at their destination on October 4, 1879, at around noon. [1] Eliza thought of the apostle Paul when he encountered a storm near the island of Crete, and was saved despite being shipwrecked. (Acts 27:1-44)

3. Kanazawa City

Kanazawa sits on very hilly terrain, with a lot of inclines within the city. Due to its mountainous geography, it must be entered by

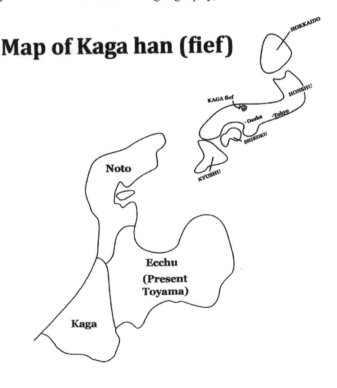

bridge over the Asano River. The river water is very clear. Beyond Kanazawa is another river, the Sai River, and the city is located between these two rivers.

Maeda was a warrior lord from about 300 years ago, who built the Kanazawa Castle on a large tract of land awarded him by his master, the Shogun. This land was a reward for all of Maeda's victories in battle. His wife was known as the "good wife and wise mother." Lord Maeda developed Kanazawa as a castle town. He invited men of letters, the literati, from Kyoto, and introduced elements of the culture in Kyoto to the community. This "Kyoto culture" included Tea Ceremony and traditional flower arrangement.

Kanazawa is surrounded by deep green conifer trees, and from the beauty and size of these trees you can tell that Kanazawa is an old city. Kanazawa Castle lies at the center of the forest, as well as a huge Japanese garden, Kenrokuen. Completed 50 years ago, the garden took 200 years to complete, and covers 25 acres. From the garden there is a beautiful view to the south of the mountain ranges.

4. The first Protestant worship services in the Hokuriku district

The Winns were able to stay at a lodging at Nagamachi 4 banchi, arranged by the Ishikawa Prefectural Government. The next day, on Sunday, October 5, 1879, Thomas and Eliza Winn held a worship service at their lodging, with their one year old baby attending.

The women who had arrived in Kanazawa with the Winns stayed at a lodge in Hikoso-machi. They included Mrs. True and her daughter Annie, and the female preacher Deguchi. The Japanese male preacher Seikichi Hayashi and his wife stayed at a rented house in Zaimoku-cho. On Friday following their arrival, the little group from Yokohama gathered together at Winn's lodging for a worship service. They thanked God for their safe arrival, and began to discuss their plans for propagating Christianity in the region. They decided that Rev. Winn would visit the Governor of Ishikawa Prefecture, and ask for permission to conduct mission work. They also delegated Rev.

Wiinn to write a letter asking for bibles, religious tracts, cards with sacred inscriptions, a type writer, as well as an organ for gatherings.

Several days later, Rev. Winn's classes in Science and English started at the Junior High Normal School. Also at about the same time, Mrs. True's English classes started. Meanwhile, Thomas Winn called on the Ishikawa Prefectural Government, and met the governor. Thomas later recalled his meeting with the governor.

> I straightforwardly stated my wish to the Governor. 'I came as a school teacher, I will faithfully carry out my duties as a Teacher. Actually though, because I am a Christian missionary, I want to do missionary work as much as possible. If I carry out missionary work in public, will the authorities interfere in it?' The Governor replied as follows: We will not interfere. There will be no interference what so ever.' I was very happy, and began to put our plans into action. [2]

The group gathered several days later at the lodge where the Winns were staying, and following their worship service, discussed their plans for preaching. They decided on the following course of action. The house next to the Winn's lodge was to be rented and gatherings were to be held there. This suggestion probably came from Eliza, who was expecting a baby. The lodge where the Winns were living was not spacious, a dark room very common in the Hokuriku district. The neighboring house had about five rooms for guests, and was big enough for gatherings.

5. Preaching begins

From this time forward, preaching could be done openly. The group made posters written in the Japanese style, in ink with brushes on Japanese paper. These were posted on the Winns' lodge and the rented house and fliers were passed out in town. Weekly Sunday services as well as daily meetings were held.

The following describes a typical church gathering in those early years in Kanazawa. The assembled people would first sing a hymn in

Japanese. Then the Japanese preacher, Seikichi Hayashi would read the Bible in Japanese. Rev. Winn would then give a sermon in Japanese explaining the section of the Bible that had been read. The version of the Bible that was read in Japanese at that time was probably *Shinyaku Zensho* (The complete New Testament) 1880, translated by Samuel R. Brown, Dr. Hepburn, and Masatsuna Okuno, or a translated version provided by Dr. Hepburn. A verse that most likely was read would have been John 3:16: "For God so loved the world that he gave His only Son, that whoever believes in him should not perish, but have eternal life."

The hymns most likely sung at the mission gathering would have included "Jesus Loves Me." This hymn was translated into Japanese by Julia Crosby, one of the founders of the Yokohama Kyoritsu Girls' School. This hymn appeared later in different hymnals, as hymn # 461 in 1954, and hymn # 464 in 1997.

> Jesus loves me! This I know,
> For the Bible tells me so.
> Little ones to Him belong;
> They are weak, but He is strong.
>
> Yes Jesus loves me!
> Yes Jesus loves me!
> Yes Jesus loves me!
> The Bible tells me so

Rev. Winn's sermon was not easy to understand for his listeners as he talked about the "salvation of Jesus Christ" to people who had never heard about the Christian faith. Moreover, although Rev. Winn most likely spoke in proper Japanese, for people who spoke the Japanese dialect of the remote area of Kanazawa, it must have been hard to understand. Despite Rev. Winn's efforts to communicate, his audience could not understand his sermon.

Despite the language barrier, both the Sunday services and the gatherings held every evening were well attended. The issue of space quickly became an issue, and Rev. Winn and his group decided to move to preacher Seikichi Hayashi's residence, which they designated as their second Gathering Hall. They soon outgrew this space as well, and in the following year were forced to move to an even larger facility, their third Gathering Hall at Shintate-machi.

The people of Kanazawa had called foreigners "ijin" (different people) and always feared foreigners, and historically had thought of them as "barbarous." Many were curious, however, at the news of this "barbarous foreigner" who had come to live in Kanazawa and spoke Japanese, and came out to see him. Although curious, very few among his early audiences were intrigued enough by his sermons to seriously consider adopting for themselves the idea of the "salvation of the sinful self."

Besides the mission gatherings, a "Sabbath School" (later called "Sunday School" and then "Church School") was established through the cooperative work of Mrs. Winn, Mrs. True, and Sei Deguchi. Parents did not initially send their children to the Sabbath School. But parents who attended the mission gatherings began to bring their children, and soon more children were attending the classes. The children were amazed to see teachers who had blue eyes different from their own dark eyes, and it was their first experience in singing hymns and listening to the stories of the Bible.

Chapter 14

Christian Evangelism and the Founding of the Aishin School

1. Home visits

Besides the regular church gatherings, both Rev. Thomas and Eliza Winn made home visits to those who attended the gatherings as well as people they met in the community. These home visits were to spread the Christian faith to the individuals and their families. A teacher who taught at the Normal School where Rev. Winn had taught wrote the following passage about the visits of the Winns, and their use of the Japanese language.

> Although Rev. and Mrs. Winn had just arrived in Japan, they did not have a great deal of trouble in using Japanese. If they did not understand certain words, they would look these up in the Japanese-English dictionary, and continue the conversation. They were able to communicate in this manner.
>
> When Rev. and Mrs. Winn came together, she seemed to have more difficulty to sit down as Rev. Winn sat sideways on the floor and did not have much space in the room for Mrs. Winn. Mrs. Winn also had trouble to adjusting to our ways of cooking food and our diet. When my aging parents were ill, she brought them food cooked according to her western methods. However the food she brought was cooked very differently from what we were accustomed to eating, and we felt bad that we could not let my parents eat this food— [1]

Early members of Kanazawa Church, 1882.
4th row: 2nd from the right, Mary True: 4th from the right,
Hachinomon Nagao; 5th from the right,
Seikichi Hayashi; 7th from the right,
Maki Nagao; 11th from the right, Thomas Clay Winn

2. The fruits of mission work

The following year, beginning in April 1880, the Winns resumed their preaching and evangelism. Seven people came forward express-ing their wish to be baptized, and the Winns led them with baptism and communion. In June of that year two additional people request-ed baptism, then four in September, and finally in December 1880 two more converted to Christianity and were baptized. The number of baptisms increased every year after that as follows: 19 in 1881, 11 in 1882, 15 in 1883, and 12 in 1884. In all there were 72 people baptized by Rev. Winn at Kanazawa Church from 1880 to 1884. Of these, 26 were women.

The social status of women in the Hokuriku district at that time was very low. Women did not have equal access with men to educa-tion. Women were not allowed to express their thoughts or feelings in public.

Given these circumstances, for a woman to "confess her faith" and receive baptism meant that they became "different," and would be looked on suspiciously by some persons. But still women were baptized in spite of encountering unfavorable conditions. Eliza Winn and Mrs. True encouraged these women with their emotional support and their own belief in the Gospel. The two women provided great encouragement for these women who were to become Christian. They did so in at least three ways. First, they modeled intelligence, knowledge and awareness in their role as women missionaries. Second, they were also seen as mothers educating their own children. Finally, they influenced these early women Christians with their own personal faith in Jesus Christ.

3. People who were baptized by Rev. Winn.

During his stay at Kanazawa [1879-1898], Rev. Winn baptized 72 people. The persons ranged in age from children receiving infant baptism, to elderly men and women who were nearly 80 years old. There were several notable individuals within this group baptized by Rev. Winn, four of whom are described below.

   a) Hachinomon Nagao. Baptized in 1880, he was originally a samurai of Kaga-han (fief) [area ranging present Ishikawa and Toyama Prefectures, Kanazawa being the capital of Kaga fief] and received an annual income of 2,030 koku of rice.[1 koku is equivalent to 5.12 bushels of rice]. In 1869, 556 Uragami Christians from the southern city of Nagasaki were banished to Kanazawa. The lord of Kaga fief at that time, Yoshiyasu Maeda, was clearing the forest to cultivate Mount Utatsu [located east of Kanazawa Castle] , and he allowed the 556 Christians to be employed there and practice their faith in Kanazawa. Then he appointed Hachinomon to be their supervisor. Hachinomon was impressed that the Christian community did not lose their spirit of love in the midst of hardship and humiliation. These Christians were later forgiven in 1873, and were allowed to return to their homes in Nagasaki. Hachinomon would come over every night to the assembly and listen intently to Rev. Winn's sermons. He thought that if the Christian religion was indeed an "evil religion" as some had described it, then it needed to be expelled right away. One evening he heard Rev. Winn preach on love as "the sword of the Bible," using as his reference the following words from 1 Corinthians 13:6-10.

> Love does not rejoice at wrong, but rejoices in the right. Love bears all things, believes all things, hopes all things, endures all things. Love never ends; as for prophecies, they will pass away; as for tongues, they will cease; as for knowledge it will pass away. For our knowledge is imperfect and our prophecy is imperfect; but when the perfect comes the imperfect will pass away.

Hearing these words, Hachinomon felt as if the scales had fallen from his eyes. He acquired land at Otemachi and constructed a building that would be used for a chapel and classrooms for the new Aishin School. He studied theology under Rev. Winn, and in 1891 was ordained and became the first elder of the Kanazawa Church. In 1886 he established the Tonomachi Church (the present day Kanazawa Motomachi Church), and worked on constructing church buildings the rest of his life.

b) Maki Nagao, the second son of Hachinomon Nagao, was a craftsman who worked with traditional Japanese paper. He heard about Christianity from his father, and was awakened to the truth of Christianity, and was baptized after his father. He studied theology for three years under Rev. Winn, and became the senior pastor at Sougawa Kogisho Assembly Hall (the present day Kashima-cho Church in Toyama Prefecture). He later preached in Komatsu, Daishoji, Gifu, and Nagoya.

c) Suenobu Sanno was baptized in 1881. He was an accomplished student of Western Studies at the Higashi Chugaku (Junior High) School. He continued his studies to become an elementary school teacher, and in that role decided that he wanted to improve his English skills. He studied English under Rev. and Mrs. Winn, and while continuing his studies in English, also studied their faith. He was converted to Christianity, was baptized, and for twelve years was an elder at the Kanazawa Church. Since he could understand English, he helped the Winns both privately and officially, and was put in charge of managing the office of the Aishin School.

Later with Eliza's suggestion and proposal, the Kanazawa Girls' School was founded by Mary Hesser, and Sanno became involved in its administration, becoming head of the School in 1894, fulfilling an important mission. As a result of his living out his Christian faith, the rest of his family members came to faith and were baptized during the period of 1882 through 1899 in Kanazawa. Sanno let Miss Kate Shaw become head of the school, succeeding after him, and he later worked for Meiji Gakuin University and became involved in students' education.

d) Cho Ishikawa was baptized in 1883 along with his wife, as well as his son's wife Tatsu, and their child Hikaru. With his baptism he became the first Protestant Christian in Toyama Prefecture. After attending the first mission gathering by Rev. Winn in Toyama Prefecture, Ishikawa said, "I am an inspector of shrines and temples, and I have always thought that Japanese religion is true religion. [2] Ishikawa experienced persecution from local people later in his life, but continued to keep his beliefs, which led to the establishment of the Sougawa Assembly Hall. His son Kumataro Ishikawa studied under the Dutch Reformed missionary, Rev. Verbeck, in Nagasaki at the age of 23. From there he stowed away on a ship bound for Shanghai in order to study "Nanga," a school of Chinese painting popular during the Edo Period (1603-1867). Kumataro was baptized

First church building, at Otemachi 2 banchi.
Also used as Aishin School.

in 1885 in Kanazawa after he returned from China. Kumataro graduated from the Tokyo Dendo Gakko (Mission School) and became the chief preacher of the Maruoka Assembly Hall in Fukui Prefecture and later became preacher at Sougawa Assembly Hall. He also provided leadership and preached at assembly halls in Shikoku and Osaka. In 1863 he returned to Kanazawa and taught at the Kanazawa Girls' School.

4. The founding of the Aishin School

The teaching contracts for both Thomas Winn and Mary True at the Normal Junior High School was to expire in September 1881. With the prospect of this expiration, Rev. and Mrs. Winn would have to return to Yokohama, but they both wished to remain in Kanazawa and continue their mission works. Thomas Winn thought that it might be possible for him to remain in Kanazawa by teaching at the private English class begun by Mary True at her lodging. His application to stay and teach was submitted to the City of Kanazawa, Ishikawa Prefecture, as well as the Foreign Ministry in Tokyo. The Prefectural authorities were the first to accept his application, so the relocation issue was resolved. Besides this, however, the prefectural authorities authorized free lodging for Rev. Winn at Nagamachi. The Prefectural government also organized a farewell party for both Rev. Winn and Mary True, and presented them each with a memorial gift. Rev. Winn was to be leaving his duties at the Normal Junior High School, and Mary True returned to teach at Shinsakae Girls' School. The Shinsakae Girls' School was to merge with the Sakurai Girls' School into the Joshi Gakuin Girls' School. With Mary's departure they abandoned their dream of founding a Women's University with a nursing department.

The question arises as to how it was that both Rev Winn and Mary True were treated so generously by the Ishikawa Prefectural government. The expression of gratitude and the positive evaluation by the Prefectural government towards these two teachers was the result of their respective personalities and good work for the community.

With the assistance of Hachinomon Nagao and Suenobu Sanno, Rev. and Mrs. Winn applied for and were granted permission for the establishment of the Aishin School, a boys' school. In the school that was subsequently founded, the two year Preparatory School, the following classes were taught: Ethics (the Bible in Japanese), Japanese language, the Chinese classics, English (reading, translation, conversation, and penmanship), history, mathematics, zoology, botany, a separate class on English grammar and composition, physics, biology, astronomy, and logic. [3]

The Aishin School was the first of its kind to teach these subjects. Twenty children were enrolled by their parents who wished for them to learn this new material.The Aishin School continued until 1899. Notable graduates who studied there for at least temporarily included Tokugoro Nakahashi, who would later go on to become Minister of Education, Kyoka Izumi, novelist, and Masaki Nakayama, who would become a professor at Meiji Gakuin University.

5. The fires at the Otemachi Church and school

In December 1882 there were fires at both the church and the school at Otemachi. Several persons entered the building, piled chairs and tables up high, and set them on fire. The fire spread immediately, but was reported immediately to Hachinomon Nagao by a soldier at the nearby Seventh Regiment in Kanazawa, who first discovered the blaze. Hachinomon immediately ran over with a neighbor and was able to extinguish the fire. Though the building was not completely burned to the ground, it could not be used after this.

Who set the fire and for what reason was never discovered. But there were people in the community at that time who were dissipated and hostile in general, and had strong feeling of fear and resentment against Christianity. There may have even been persons jealous that the children attending the higher school were from wealthy families.

Rev. and Mrs. Winn quickly held a discussion with church elders such as Hachinomon Nagao and Suenobu Sanno to rebuild the church and school. By the following February, funds sent from the Board of Foreign Missions of Presbyterian Church (North)in the United States arrived. Adding to this their own donations as well as those from other sources, church leaders were able to acquire a piece of land and secure a building in Tonomachi, and began to use this as a temporary church and school building.

6. The oldest Christian kindergarten existing in Japan

In 1881, Rev. Winn contacted James B. Porter, a missionary from the United States, to come to Japan, and the following year invited him to Kanazawa and asked him to take over the management of the Aishin School. James Porter subsequently helped operate and develop the school for the following six years. In 1885, Porter changed the name of the school to the Hokuriku Eiwa (English) School, and then moved the school's location to Hirosaka Street, and then to Kodatsuno. In 1888 Porter was transferred to Osaka by his mission board and began to preach in the Kansai [Kobe-Osaka-Kyoto] district.

Rev. and Mrs. Winn had for many years requested the Board of Foreign Missions of Presbyterian Church (North) in the United States to send medical missionaries. The following year James Porter arrived in Kanazawa, the Woman's Presbyterian Board of Missions in Chicago sent Sarah K. Cummings, a woman medical missionary, to Kanazawa .The following year in 1884, she and James B. Porter were married, and she continued her medical practice. In 1887, however, the Japanese government advised her to stop her medical practice, as she did not have a Japanese medical license. So she decided to help at her husband's school. [4] She was the first woman medical missionary to be sent to Japan.

James Porter heard in 1881 that his sister Francina E. Porter had been assigned as a woman missionary. The following year his brother arrived, and she came to Japan as well. She was a very active woman, who had graduated from the School of Education at the Presbyterian Maryville University. Following a discussion with Rev. and Mrs. Winn, she and her brother James Porter, and Mary Hesser founded the Eiwa Elementary School and Eiwa Kindergarten in January 1886 in a rented house. Then in September 1889 they were able to move into a new building at Shimohonda-machi for the Elementary School and Kindergarten with funds provided by the Presbyterian Churches in Philadelphia combined with what they had raised locally. As a result of this teaching of children in the community, interest in nursery education increased. Following the issuance of the Private School Edict [issued in July 1899 by the Japanese Government] the Aishin School and the Eiwa Elementary School were closed. However the Eiwa Kindergarten still exists today, as an institution attached to the Hokuriku Gakuin Junior College. It is the oldest Christian kindergarten still in existence in Japan today.

Chapter 15

The Establishment of the Kanazawa Church, and Mission Trips to Noto and Toyama

1. Submitting an application for the establishment of the Kanazawa Church

Between the months of April and September, 1880, Rev. Winn baptized thirteen people. The thirteen who were baptized then submitted an "Application for Establishing the Kanazawa Church" to the Japan Christian Union Church [First Protestant Church in Japan founded in 1872 in Yokohama by Presbyterian and Dutch Reformed Churches]. The Presbytery held at Tokyo Kyobashi Church reviewed the application, and subsequently approved the establishment of the Kanazawa Church. There were Japanese clergy at that time in the early history of the Japan Christian Union Church. If the church could identify a tentative Japanese clergy assignment, along with the name of a foreign missionary and the election of deacons and elders, the establishment of a church was routinely accepted.

However, the establishment of the Kanazawa Church was postponed [for seven months. Members of the Presbytery's Building Committee for establishing Kanazawa Church thought it was too early to build the church. Also it was difficult to get a qualified Japanese pastor. Rev. Winn asked the representative members of the Presbytery to cooperate, so he went to Yokohama, Tokyo, and also asked for help for the representatives in Kyushu. While he was away for 6 months, Rev. Thomas Alexander stayed in Kanazawa.]. In May, 1881, the consecration service for the new building was held at the temporary chapel in Otemachi. About one hundred people in all attended the ceremony, which included Rev. Thomas Winn, Rev. Thomas Alexander, Rev. Shozaburo Aoyama, then pastor of Shimonoseki Akamagasaki Church, Chuei Aoki, elder of Tokyo Rogetsu-cho Church, Preacher Seikichi Hayashi, and women missionaries Eliza Winn and Mary True. Four people were baptized on this occasion. Hachinomon Nagao was ordained an elder, and others were ordained deacons. The Kanazawa Church was at this ceremony formally established. The spirits of those early church members must have been high. Rev. Winn wrote to the Board of Foreign Missions of the Presbyterian Church in the United States celebrating the establishment of the Kanazawa Church, saying "I am glad to report that the members of this little church manifest very commendable zeal in trying to carry the Gospel to others." [1]

2. The Missions to Nanao, Toyama, Takaoka, and Isurugi

The passion for mission outreach was very high in this young congregation. In August, 1881, several members of the Kanazawa Church became excited about going on a mission trip to Noto, and Toyama [Please refer to the Map of Hokuriku District]. A mission group was formed consisting of Rev. Winn, the deacon Satoru Kato, the divinity student Chuei Aoki, and Daigen Nishimura, a member of the newly formed Kanazawa Church. They first headed to Nanao [northern city in Ishikawa Prefecture, located near Noto Peninsula, refer the map], where for two consecutive nights the group led a mission gathering for the community. Each night the attendance exceeded 100 persons, with the total for both nights approximating 260 people.

The mission group left the day following their last mission gathering, and travelled by ship to the town of Fushiki. They started

MAP OF HOKURIKU DISTRICT:
Related Places of Winn's Mission

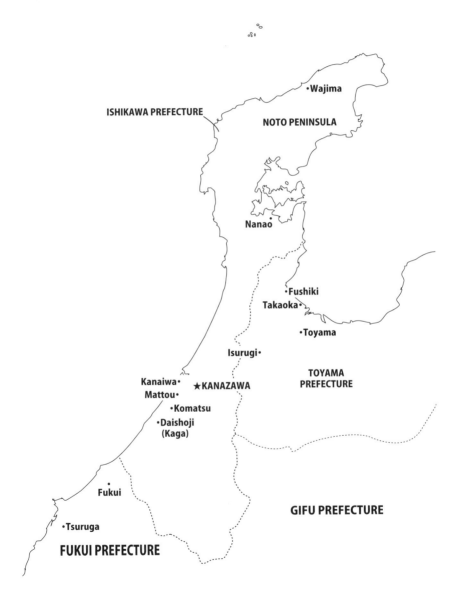

preaching as they had in Nanao, but their meeting was interrupted by people throwing rocks and dirt at them. As a result they left Fushiki, and went on to Toyama.

On August 11, 1881, the group arrived at Toyoma and resumed their mission outreach work. In the afternoon gathering on that day, 80 people attended, and in the evening session 110 were gathered. On Sunday morning, August 14, four members of the mission group led a worship service. There were 100 in attendance at the afternoon gathering, and in the evening the total number present reached 300.

At the close of the afternoon gathering, a white-haired gentleman came forward to visit the mission group. He introduced himself as Cho Ishikawa, and he became the first Protestant believer in Toyama. His son Kumataro Ishikawa, influenced by his father, later became a preacher [in Toyama, Osaka, and Shikoku] .

However there were those in Toyama who were unhappy about the arrival of the new Christian mission group. The Otani sect of the Buddhist Honganji lecture centers had been promoted to the status of Branch Temple in September, 1844. However the new preaching missionaries of the Christian church were so devout that they became a great hindrance to the temple being able to spread Buddhism. So the Branch Temple decided to start an anti-Christian campaign. They sent a spy to the first mission gathering, trying to find negative aspects to the Christian faith. From the information provided by their informant, the Temple officials created a "Counting Song," critical of Christianity. On the day of the mission outreach events [August 14] the local Buddhist temple passed out fliers attacking Christianity, with the words of the song printed on them. These were handed to those who had come to pray at the temple. The song was in the form of a counting series beginning with the number one, with other numbers in succession, although some numbers were missing. The words to the song are as follows.

One....In this wild world Christ spreads evil religion and deceives the world. O how sinful.

Two...Buddhism does not exist in two, brightens up the world with true light, oh how thankful.

Three...Just seeing the cross is disgraceful, and how can you pray for happiness, don't talk nonsense.

Nine...Oh how stubborn are Christians, not thinking of the Land of Lord; you are traitors of our nation.

Eleven...Though how much you read the Bible, it is heretical and has many flaws. What a pity.

Thirteen...Finally, facing the end, Christ calls out for God not saving Him. What a fool.

Seventeen...Alone on the mountain path leading to death, Christians walk along and cry, going to hell.

Nineteen...Christians lead this country in a mistaken direction, and Japanese will get rid of them. Oh they are patriots.

This is how Buddhists criticized and slandered Christians. When Buddhist believers heard the words of the song, they seemed to get a lot of enjoyment from them. [2] On August 16, four from the mission group including Rev. Winn met to lead a meeting. They found a place for the gathering, and over 60 people showed up to attend. But when the meeting was about to start, the owner of the gathering place refused to let them stay, and they reluctantly cancelled the meeting. The gathering had been reported to the police, and was moved to another location. Mission meetings were subsequently held on August 18 and 19. However these meetings became very noisy due to many interruptions, including persons throwing ceramic tiles and stones at the participants, as well as showering them with all manner of verbal abuse. By the time that the gathering had ended, Rev. Winn had had mud poured over his head. The crowd tried to throw the divinity student Chuei Aoki into the river, but he was fortunate enough to somehow escape. [3]

This event was followed on August 21 by a mission outreach meeting at Isurugi. There were 30 people in attendance at the afternoon gathering, but 300 people showed up for the evening meeting.

Those who came to attend the evening meeting walked over the fragile tatami flooring with their street shoes, and in the uproar that followed in the assembly hall, the floor collapsed and the gathering had to be abruptly cancelled. Despite these setbacks, the gathering took place the following day at the same place in the afternoon and evening. There were 80 attending in the afternoon and 80 people attended the evening sessions, throughout the day, with about 80 people for each of the afternoon and evening sessions. Thus about 500 people attended the gathering at Isurugi on Augustu 21.

Although there was never any direct threat to Mrs. Winn and her baby, there were children who followed them and circled them with strange noises and dance gestures. There was never any attempt to harm them, as the Japanese regarded foreigners as somehow special. But Eliza was worried more about the safety of her husband Rev. Winn and the other preachers in the group. Persecution of foreign religion could be severe in Japan, and Eliza recalled the biblical scene of Paul preaching to the Gentiles and facing death, and Stephen who was persecuted and died as a martyr. She took comfort in the words from Isaiah 53:3, knowing that they were taking part in the biblical tradition of suffering for the sake of their faith: "He was despised and rejected by men; a man of sorrows, and acquainted with grief;" Rev. and Eliza Winn prayed that their mission would be carried out and that God would bless them as they spread the Gospel.

Chapter 16

Development of Mission and Storm of Persecution

1. Various experiences of obstructing preaching and intensified persecution of mission work

Though there were only a few members at the new Kanazawa Church, "each of these men and women is a match for a thousand." Their mission work centered on the Kanazawa Church and Assembly Hall, and spread throughout the Hokuriku district. But as their preaching spread and gained in popularity, it aggravated a growing conflict with the established religious institutions in the region. This conflict grew into an overt obstruction of events, and persecution of participants. The Hokuriku district was a very conservative region, clinging to the old traditions from their Buddhist heritage. The national culture at that time was accepting of the "westernization of the nation," but in that region the idea of accepting the foreign religion of Christianity was "a matter of life or death."

Those who converted to Christianity in many cases had to cease their relationship with their family and forever break ties with friends and acquaintances. It was perhaps natural for these recent converts to Christianity to be despised by others in the community. For a believer to become a Christian meant to convert from Buddhism. This meant that the convert would have to turn down the belief of a religion that had continued for generations. The Hokuriku district was a traditional center of Buddhism in Japan. The Jodo Shinshu sect of Buddhism prevailed there, and with the influence of Priest Rennyo, the Jodo Buddhist beliefs had prevailed for over 600 years. Buddhists thought that the foreigners were using "strange words" when they preached the "Gospel," and talked about the "Holy Spirit" and the importance of "Love." Those who followed Buddhist teachings were often made uncomfortable by this new language and theology, and a few of them became active in persecuting and hindering the Christian missionaries.

In August 1881, Rev. Winn had scheduled meetings with Seikichi Hayashi and other members of the Kanazawa Church in the towns of Mattou, Komatsu, and Daishoji. When they arrived at Daishoji they discovered that the site of one of their recent meetings was closed. When they asked why the house was closed, it was explained that many people with spears had come and drove the owner of the house outside.

This was also the year that Rev. Winn and members of the church held evangelical meetings for three days at the town of Takaoka. During that time they were subject to countless attacks by hoodlums, who threw stones at them, swore and screamed at them, and chased them with spears. Rev. Winn ran through dark alleys as fast as he could, and barely avoided injury.

There were several accounts of bravery among the small Christian community at this time. A new believer named Daigen Nishimura was baptized early in 1880. He was a Chinese medical doctor, but lost his job when he became a Christian, and had to make a living selling Bibles.

The preacher Toshiyuki Kato was known as a brave but gentle person. He came to the Hokuriku district from Tokyo to preach in the community. One summer night in 1883, walking home along a remote road after visiting church members, he was attacked by two hoodlums. The blood ran from a wound on his head and spilled on the Bible he was carrying under his arms. He could not fight back but fell down on the ground. The hoodlums attacked him repeatedly, hitting him in the head and torso, and left him lying there on the ground. Kato somehow managed to crawl the rest of his way back home. Kato returned to Tokyo following this incident in order to recover from his injuries, but died the following May. Kato became the first martyr in the Hokuriku district.

2. Various experiences

From 1877 through 1883, Rev. and Mrs. Winn had many different experiences of both sadness and joy. In August 1878, their oldest daughter Mary was born, and in November 1879, their oldest son Willard was born. Another time of joy took place when, in the autumn of 1880, Eliza's brother Matthew and their mother Mrs. Cordelia Willard came to Japan and stayed with the Winns until the following spring. Then a time of both joy and sadness followed: in July 1882 their second son George was born, but in the following month their oldest son Willard passed away. Reflecting on this sad time in their lives, Thomas Winn commented as follows, recorded in Shoshichi Nakazawa's *Nihon no Shito: Thomas Winn Den* (Disciple of Japan: Life of Thomas C. Winn).

> Willard developed a high fever, and on August 1st he passed away. I let him sleep by his mother and let her see him as much as possible. When I was travelling with my wife Eliza to Osaka in September to address her health concerns, I myself suffered an acute headache, which did not go away. On September 25th, I gave a sermon in the morning and I was going to give another sermon in the afternoon, but I could not bear the pain. I could not give the sermon, but instead laid on a couch, tied my head with a handkerchief, and tried to withstand the pain. I could not remember anything that happened that month, and I learned later that I had contracted typhoid fever. Willard my son had contracted typhoid fever, and I was probably also affected.
>
> People in Osaka were very kind to us. At that time, there weren't any trained nurses available, so our friends tried their best to take

care of me in shifts that went through the night. My wife Eliza had to take care of me as well, and look after the newborn baby. So she had a very difficult time for several weeks. [1]

Rev. Winn recovered somewhat from his illness, and at his doctor's suggestion was hospitalized in Tokyo. By March 1883, his health had improved, and he went first to Osaka and then returned to Kanazawa.

Chapter 17

The Founding of the Kanazawa Girls' School

1. The Story of Emma Willard

Persecution of Christians persisted over the years that the Winns stayed in Kanazawa. Rev. Winn was interrupted while he was preaching in the community, and church members encountered persecution when they were outside their meeting room. Even Eliza and her children were affected. Their neighbors as well as people they met for the first time would stare at them and give them strange looks. People who passed by the church with their children would yell out slanderous words.

Rev. and Mrs. Winn had been aware of the reality of this situation before their arrival, for the religious situation was exactly what they had heard from Dr. Hepburn before they left for Kanazawa. In general, he told them the Japanese people practiced animism and pantheism, and were not interested in what westerners considered to be religion, and therefore had trouble understanding these concepts. It was difficult for Japanese people to understand and believe in the God of Christianity, or practice the Christian faith. Rev. and Eliza Winn wondered why this was so. They wondered why in Japanese culture there didn't appear to be a sense of awe and respect for the absolute Power of the Christian God.

Eliza was reminded of a story told to her many years earlier by her grandfather Matthew Chambers, about Middlebury, Vermont. The situation back then might be similar to the one in Japan, she thought. Eliza and Thomas had already founded the Boys' School, "Aishin Gakko,"[The term "Aishin School" will be used in this book] and were teaching there. This Aishin School was successful. Their students were studying very hard, and their prospects for the future were bright, and full of hope. As a result of this success, Eliza became hopeful that it would be possible to found a school to educate girls in the area. Eliza had heard the name of Emma Willard from her grandfather, and possibly had researched her biography at the library of Knox College while she attended there. Emma Willard had a strong idea of what was needed at that time, and made a proposal ["A plan for Improving Female Education" was presented to the members of New York Legislature in1819]. Emma felt strongly that young girls would need an education in fine literature and the natural sciences if they were to know the basics of Christianity and Ethics, learn academic methods, and manage their families.

Around June 1881, Eliza shared with her husband Thomas her ideas of establishing a Girls' School in Kanazawa, and he agreed. Thomas passed on to Eliza the information he had received from Rev. Thomas Alexander that the Woman's Presbyterian Board of Missions of the Northwest in Chicago would be sending two women missionaries to Osaka or Kanazawa.

On July 20, 1881, Rev. Thomas Winn wrote a letter to Dr. John Lowrie of the Board of Foreign Missions of the Presbyterian Church in New York. This letter led to the founding of the Kanazawa Girls' School, inspired by Eliza Winn's ideas.

> Another thing of which I wish to speak is about the sending of young ladies to assist in the work at Kanazawa. If any are sent they must be ladies of some experience or they will not be able to do anything in the way of establishing a girls' school. I think that if the right persons came they would be able to build up a school for girls. I understand that two quite young ladies from Chicago have been offered

Mary Hesser

for the Kanazawa work. If they should come I trust that their work will be eminently successful. But I want to repeat that the beginning of such a work as is proposed needs persons of experience. [2]

2. The Interview with Mary Hesser

One of the young ladies from Chicago sent by the Chicago Women's Board of Missions was Mary Hesser. Eliza and Thomas Winn first met the female missionary, Mary Hesser, on the morning of April 25, 1883, when they were staying at the Kawaguchi Foreign Settlement. Rev. Winn had been attending the Presbytery ("Chukai") meeting held in Nagasaki [a long way from Kanazawa] . He was scheduled to participate in the Mission Advisory Board Meeting in the afternoon of April 25, and planned to return to Kanazawa a few days later with his family.

Mary Hesser came to visit Thomas and Eliza by herself. After their introductions, she asked them to provide more information about the Girls' School in Kanazawa, as she had heard about it from Rev. Alexander. Rev. Winn had known about the two women missionaries from Chicago, and had expressed his wish to meet with them at the Mission Advisory Board Meeting before they returned to Kanazawa. He explained that the establishment of the Girls' School had been planned by his wife, Eliza. He told Mary that in order for this plan to be successful, it was necessary for her to know about the community of Kanazawa. He wanted her to know the geographic environment, the historical background, and the religious situation in the community where they were considering establishing the Girls' School. Mary listened intently, and although she asked few questions she most likely understood the challenge very well.

3. Mary Hesser's Personal Resume

When Rev. Winn was finished with his explanations, and Mary had asked her questions, Rev. and Mrs. Winn reviewed Mary's resume with her. Rev. Alexander had forwarded them a copy of her resume which listed the following personal information and work history.

1) July 1853. Born in Pennsylvania as daughter of Catholic German immigrant father, who was a furniture craftsman
2) September 1859: Studied at Catholic School for six years and graduated from there
3) September 1865: Studied at the Free School for two years
4) 1867-78: Helped at home, worked as a dress maker at a shop in Erie
5) September 1878: For four years, studied at Western Female Seminary, Oxford, Ohio, established under the Holyoke Plan. She attended the Presbyterian Church, and in December 1879, made her "Confession of Faith" at the Presbyterian Church.
6) June 1882: Assigned as a Woman Missionary to Japan by the Board of Foreign Missions of the Presbyterian Church (North) in the United States.

7) October 1882: The Missionary Association Assignment Plan for Women Missionaries in Japan requested her assignment by both the Board of Foreign Missions of the Presbyterian Church in the United States (North) and the Chicago Woman's Presbyterian Board of Missions. This request was accepted, and Mary came to Japan via Yokohama to the Kawaguchi Foreign Concession in Osaka. At the Concession she helped Rev. Thomas Winn's friend, Rev. Alexander, for six months in preaching, and awaiting the establishment of a Girls' School somewhere in Japan.

4. Mary Hesser's actual practice in Kanazawa

Mary's meeting with Rev. and Mrs. Winn was completed on that afternoon [of April 25, 1883.] The following afternoon, Rev. Alexander gave a report to the Advisory Committee, and later sent the following message to the Board of Foreign Missions of the Presbyterian Church (North) in the United States.

> Messrs Winns and Porter and I advised Miss Hesser to remain in Osaka. We made it a mistake for her to go to Kanazawa. She insisted that the Lord was leading her and that was right to follow His leading rather than that of her own. We are aware that sometimes,
> "Lord moves in mysterious way
> His wonders to perform";
> Therefore we are doubtful about this case. But we'd make the best of this dispensation. [3]

Since these comments had been made, the Committee decided to delay the decision to require that Mary first remain in Osaka. They instead decided to let her go to Kanazawa and become directly involved in mission work there.

In late April Mary left Osaka with the Winns, and began the long journey to Kanazawa. They went by train from Osaka to Kyoto, and continued on to Otsu by rickshaw. The journey from Otsu to Shiotsu, located on the northern part of Lake Biwa, was made by steam ship, and from Shiotsu to Tsuruga by palanquin. From Tsuruga they were able to take another steam ship, stopping first at the port of Hashidate before finally reaching the port of Kanazawa.

Mary stayed at the Winn's house for 5 months while she prepared for her new role in Kanazawa. She helped with Rev. Winn's mission work, taught at the Aishin School for Boys, and studied the Japanese language. She also prepared herself for the establishment of the Girls' School in Kanazawa, wrote a report on her stay at Kanazawa, and presented this report to the Advisory Committee.

Mary witnessed Rev. Winn and other members dedicating their lives to Christian mission. She also experienced the faith of the members of the Kanazawa Church. She saw the obstacles put up by people in the community, as well as violent opposition of some persons to the mission work. She also was able to experience firsthand the seriousness and earnestness of the students at Aishin School. Mary learned form Eliza many things about Japan, including the fact that the social position of women was subservient to men, and how the education of girls was inadequate. Members of the Christian churches were very protective of Mary, and attentive to her needs. An elder in the church, Sanno-san, understood English and was especially helpful in many different situations, for which Mary was very grateful.

When Mary's internship at Kanazawa was approaching its close, Mary confirmed with Eliza that the education of girls was both necessary and important. Mary informed Eliza in considering the educational method to be used, that she thought that the Holyoke Plan practiced at her alma mater would be appropriate. When Mary gave her presentation, she mentioned her research on Emma Willard, which had special meaning for Eliza.

5. Establishment of the Kanazawa Girls' School

Mary met with Rev. Alexander in October, 1883 and presented him with her report on her internship in Kanazawa. After reading her

Kanazawa Girls' School at Kami Kakibatake

report, Rev. Alexander informed her that he had also received a positive report about her work from Rev. Winn. Rev. Alexander then discussed her assignment to Kanazawa, and told her that she had been approved by the committee and gave her encouragement for her work.

She began immediately to use her contacts in the Kobe and Osaka area to try and find an appropriate Japanese head as well as full time teachers. She also decided which textbooks were to be used at the school, and ordered them.

Mary returned to Kanazawa in late October. Her first order of business was to decide on a name for the school for girls. She consulted with the Elders of Kanazawa Church, as well as with Rev. and Mrs. Winn. It was decided after these consultations that the name of the school would be "Kanazawa Girls' School!' There were no objections to this decision. At that time there were not any public schools for girls in Kanazawa.

Mary lived temporarily on Hirosaka Street in Kanazawa where she opened her own "Hesser's School." She began teaching English to four girls at the request of their parents. This small school marked the true beginning of girls' education in the Hokuriku district, and was the origin of Hokuriku Gakuin.

After many twists and turns, the Japanese head of the new school and the full time teachers were appointed. The head and full

**Organ played by Eliza Winn at the Opening ceremony
of Kanazawa Girls' School**

time teachers' proposal, "An Inquiry into the Establishment of the Kanazawa Girls' School," was presented to the Ishikawa Prefectural government in February 1885, and it was approved.

Once the church received the approval, a vacant lot near Hesser's School was found in April, 1885. The site for the new school was purchased under the names of three church members: Maki Nagao, Suenobu Sanno, and Chuei Aoki, and construction started. The Board of Foreign Missions of the Presbyterian Church (North) in the United States financed the entire cost of the acquisition of the land as well as the construction of the school building. However these accomplishments were all the result of the great effort expended by Rev. Winn.

The opening ceremony of the Kanazawa Girl's School took place on September 9, 1885, with the ringing of a bell. Accompanied by Eliza Winn playing the organ, 23 students sang a hymn. After a greeting was given by the governor of the prefecture, Mary Hesser gave a speech.

As there is a saying that women raising children govern the world, the education of women is as important as a man's. In the education

First students and staffs of Kanazawa Girls' School

of women, both physical and moral knowledge are important. With general education based on Christianity, it is necessary to enlighten and nurture the religious beliefs of students. Thus our goal of establishing this school will be fulfilled through a general education based on Christianity. We hope to build up the good character of our students, which will shine through in good times and bad. [4]

With the establishment of the Girls' School that day, Eliza Winn's dream had come true. She had long thought of establishing a school for girls, and so this celebration was very emotional for her.

With the opening of the Girls' School, both Eliza and Thomas Winn supported the school in all aspects and played a great part in its development. Mary Hesser could not play the organ well, so Eliza taught music classes. Regarding the equipment and facilities of the school, for example, Rev. and Mrs. Winn donated a large sum of money, 1,000 yen [equivalent to roughly today's 3million yen, US$30,000], which funded the building of a second story which could also be used as a chapel.

Chapter 18

Construction of a Building Leading to an Independent Tonomachi Church

1. Construction of a church building

A house and surrounding land were purchased in February 1883, with the goal of using it for both the temporary hall for the Kanazawa Church and the school building for the Aishin School. In November of that year Rev. Porter arrived in Kanazawa and was asked to be in charge of the administration of the school.

Many of the members of the church had voiced strong support for the construction of a church building, and the elders designed a plan which was then approved by the congregation's General Assembly. This approval guaranteed the wholehearted cooperation of the congregation and led to the request for donations. A vacant lot in Otemachi was located and purchased, and construction began. However in mid-process it was determined that the land was not appropriate [Otemachi was located near Kanazawa Castle and was the center of the City during the Edo Period (1603-1867). However, as the Prefectural government Office was located on Hirosaka Street, the Church decided to move to Ishiura-machi to be the central area in Kanazawa City], and another lot was found and purchased that was in the center of the city, facing the main road in Ishiura-machi. Construction was resumed at this new location. The church building was completed in November 1884, and the fund raising mainly relied on offerings of the Church members. Looking back at the decision to change the location of the church building, considering the later development of Kanazawa, it was a wise and brave decision to move the site in mid-process. [1]

The church building was financed in the following way. Rev. and Mrs. Winn gave a donation, which allowed for the purchase of the land. One-third of the cost of construction was paid by through the sale of the "Oshie" which was raised cloth pictures designed by Mrs. Winn and made by the women members of the church. At the dedication of the new church building, hymns were sung with Mrs. Winn's organ accompaniment. Rev. Winn preached in Japanese. The service was attended by 200 people. Not all could be accommodated, and some had to stand outside the hall.

2. The Goal of an Independent Church

The construction of the new building led to the church's independence with a Japanese pastor. Rev. Winn had always encouraged the congregation towards the goal of independence in his regular requests for offerings, and in his statements of this goal "to aim to establish an independent church" in fact this was also actually the policy of the Board of Foreign Missions of the Presbyterian Church (North) in the United States. This independence of the new congregation was also what Dr. Hepburn had discussed, and that Rev. and Eliza Winn wished to implement.

The Kanazawa Church decided to appoint Chuei Aoki as its first pastor. Chuei Aoki had come from Tokyo in May 1881, and had attended the formation of the original church hall. Later on as a divinity student, he had accompanied Rev. Winn's Christian mission to Noto and Toyama districts. Members of the congregation felt that he was the right person, both in his faith and his personality. Chuei Aoki was formally approved as the pastor of the Kanazawa Church at the meeting of the Naniwa Chukai (Presbytery). The Presbytery in this way acknowledged the Kanazawa Church as an Independent Church.

Chuei Aoki, first pastor of the Kanazawa Church

The organization of the church consisted of 3 elders, 2 deacons, and 76 members including 38 members with their families. The membership was not very large, but they had a strong faith, lived humbly, and gave generous offerings which managed to sustain their church by itself.

With their new church building recently constructed, and having received a Japanese pastor, the commitment of this church to the burning flame of mission expanded. In November, an assembly hall was built in Komatsu. Rev. Winn, the new pastor Chuei Aoki, and other elders [of the Kanazawa Church] attended the gathering, and shared their faith with those in attendance.

3. The Construction of the Tonomachi Church

The challenges faced by the early members of the Tonomachi Church are described in an account found in 80 Years of Kanazawa Hikoso Church (*Kanazawa Hikoso Kyokai 80 nen-shi*), and A Brief History of Tonomachi Church (*Tonomachi Kyokai Ryakushi*). This early history is described as follows.

Kanazawa City is long and narrow: long in its dimension from east to west, and narrow going north to south. The Sai River flows through the western part of the city, and the Asano River flows in the east. Kodatsuno Hill rises from the plain on which the city was built, and on this plain a castle was built and stands out at the center of the city. Geography not only affects the characteristics and culture of Kanazawa, but splitting the city into two parts makes travel difficult. In order for the city to be accessible it developed into two distinct parts. These factors were considered in the building of the Tonomachi Church. [2]

When the new building for the Kanazawa Church was constructed, 13 members of the church established an assembly hall in the eastern part of the city, and requested the elders of the church that worship services be held there. Rev. Winn discussed this proposal with the church elders who approved the plan as a church session. Kanaya-machi Assembly Hall was in this manner established in the eastern part of the city. In the book, A Brief History of Tonomachi Church, the extraordinary devotion to spreading the Christian faith is record-ed as follows.

> Rev. Porter "has developed the Assembly Hall in Kanayamachi, and spread the Gospel at that location. There were many who came seeking the Way. It was thought that an opportunity to spread the Gospel must not be lost. Now a separate church has been established in the eastern part of the city. If a spiritual fire is set in both the eastern and western parts of the city, a much larger fire may burst into flames and consume the entire city. [3]

The Presbytery meeting, the Naniwa Chukai, was held at the Kanazawa Church in October 1886. The Presbytery approved the es-tablishment of the Tonomachi Japan Church of Christ. The congre-gation held a dedication ceremony for the new building. At the Gen-eral Meeting which followed Maki Nagao was elected Elder and also appointed a deacon for the church. Immediately after this election, there was a worship service with the sacrament of communion, and

Maki Nagao was ordained as the head minister. The preceding account is a description of the founding of the Tonomachi Church, now known as Motomachi Church.

In its later history, Tonomachi Church grew unexpectedly and there was a desire to expand into a church hall. The church made a request for donations, and subsequently purchased property in Nakamachi. The new building was constructed, and the dedication ceremony for the new church hall was held in April 1889.

4. Thomas has to return to the United States following an injury to his eye

While the churches were growing and making progress, Rev. Winn experienced a personal setback that was to affect his work with them. In January 1886, Rev. Winn took part in a playful snowball fight with students of the Hokuriku Eiwa School. Just as he was turning away, a snowball hit him in the right eye. He felt acute pain, and lost sight in his right eye. He went immediately to the Prefectural Hospital, where he was diagnosed as having a cerebral hemorrhage of the eyes. He was told at that point that it was not possible to have appropriate treatment at that hospital.

He discussed his options with Eliza, and decided to see a noted ophthalmologist in Kobe. This physician suggested that Rev. Winn return to the United States, and receive proper treatment and get some rest. Missionaries at that time were entitled to a year furlough after 8 years of service in the field, and so using this benefit, Rev. Winn and his family returned to the United States.

Just as they were about to leave from Yokohama, they received a telegram from their home in Galesburg [Illinois] with the news that "Mother has passed away." Thomas regretted that he had not returned sooner, as he would have had one last visit with his mother.

The voyage across the Pacific Ocean was calm despite it being winter, but Thomas and Eliza were sunk deep in sorrow. They made the return to Galesburg after a long journey. Thomas, Eliza and their children paid a visit to his mother's grave.

After some time had passed, Thomas went to see a doctor in Chicago. The doctor told him to rest quietly for one year. So Thomas rested and tried to recover, but when his condition began to improve a little, he began to help his brother George at the flour mill.

One day, on the way back from delivering flour, and riding a horse drawn carriage down a slope, a part of one of the wheels broke off. The horse was startled and jumped high, kicking Thomas' thigh hard. To make matters worse, Thomas was thrown down from the coach driver's box, and his left leg hit the ground hard. There wasn't any hospital nearby, nor any telephone to call for help. Thomas did not know what to do. Fortunately, a young man working on a farm nearby saw what was happening and came to help. Calling another man, the two of them managed to carry Thomas to a hospital. He had a great deal of bleeding, and had a partial bone fracture on his left hand.

Because of the accident, Thomas had to remain in bed for half a year, from July through December. He was not even able to walk on crutches. Also because of his severe bleeding, he experienced pain in his right eye. It must have been very hard for Eliza to take care of him all that time. Consequently most of their furlough was spent in Thomas' treatment and recovery.

5. The Change of Pastors, the completion of the Mission Station, and the birth of their third son

The Winns left Galesburg in July 1886, returning to Japan and their mission in Kanazawa. There were three matters which concerned Rev. Winn, but they were all resolved in the year that followed.

The first matter was the successful change of pastors at Kanazawa Church. Their first pastor, Chuei Aoki had been called by the Osaka Minami Church, and transferred to Osaka. In November the Kanazawa Church welcomed the succeeding pastor, Kaichi Banno.

Kanazawa Foreign Mission Station

The second matter concerned on the use of the western style building that was completed at Kodatsuno with Eliza's help. The new
building was to be a Mission Station, that is, the headquarters for the
Hokuriku district. It was to be used for district Presbytery meetings.
It was also actually used as a temporary residence for visiting missionaries. When Dr. Arthur Mitchell, a board member of the Board
of Foreign Missions of the Presbyterian Church in the United States,
came to Kanazawa to give a talk, he stayed at this building. In October of that same year, when the Kanazawa Church held a regional
Presbytery (Naniwa Chukai) meeting at their church, all of the missionaries who attended the gathering stayed at this "Station." Eliza
was in charge of taking care of them.

The third matter was a happy one concerning the birth of their
third son Merle soon after moving into the new building.

6. Singing from the New Hymnal (*Shinsen Sambika*)

The resolution of a third issue also brought satisfaction to Eliza,
and this was the publication in 1888 of the *Shinsen Sambika*. This

hymnal contained only the lyrics; a hymnal with the musical scores was to be published in 1890. This hymnal was the product of a joint project of the Japanese Presbyterian and Congregational Churches, following discussions on the need for a hymnal published in Japanese. The hymnal committee included Masatsuna Okuno, as well as members of a committee that had been translating the Old Testament: Takakichi Matsunaga, Masahisa Uemura. Rev. George Allchin (1852-1935) who was well versed in music, edited this hymnal, which was regarded as the most well organized hymnal ever published. Eliza sang several songs from this hymnal and approved of all of them. The literary style of the *Shinsen Sambika* was progressive poetry. The hymns were orthodox in spirit, reflecting an open and deeply spiritual expression of faith. [4]

Eliza's favorite hymn "Lord, I hear of showers of blessing," was translated into Japanese (translated by Masatsuna Okuno, *Shinsen Sambika* #162). Eliza would play this hymn at the services of the Kanazawa Church and the Tonomachi Church, and at times at the worship services of the Kanazawa Girls' School. Feeling a sense of happiness overwhelm her, she would sing in praise of God.

Chapter 19

The Church Building Collapses, and the Church Faces Challenges of Maintaining Its Independent Status

1. The Collapse of the Church Building and Reconstruction

In January 1891 there was a great snowstorm in the Hokuriku District. The Kanazawa Church building collapsed under the weight of the heavy snow. It was completely crushed, and the chairs and the organ were shattered into pieces. The building had been in existence for only 8 years.

Kanazawa's local newspaper reported: "Christian Church collapsed under heavy snow." Using a play on words in Japanese, where the word "*mendo*" means "a lot of trouble," the paper concluded the article with the phrase "*A-mendo*." Those with anti-Christian sentiments cried out openly that "O Christianity has collapsed, O Christianity has collapsed."

At the Kanazawa Church Session that followed it was decided to hold services at the hall of the Kanazawa Girls' School, and at other places. The Session also voted to rebuild the church building. After consulting with its members, the church was able to purchase an adjacent lot. In so doing the church doubled the area where it was to rebuild.

The entire cost of reconstruction amounted to 1,350 yen. This amount was covered in a manner similar to when the original church building was constructed. Offerings came from church members, as well as from donations from within Japan and abroad. For this construction, Rev. and Mrs. Winn gave an offering of 200 yen, an enormous amount for that time.

The true story of Masataro Atoji who was baptized in 1888 is by now well known to everyone, but must be told here. He had been an elder of the church, and was head of the Eiwa Elementary School. He consulted with his wife, who had been baptized a year earlier, in 1889, as to whether or not he should donate 10 yen towards the reconstruction of the church building. His actual salary was 8 yen per month. One month after he had spoken with his wife, Pastor Banno paid a visit to their home, and asked the amount of his pledge towards the new building. He said that he would donate 20 yen. His wife was astonished, but he had thought of a good way to increase his pledge. He had learned how to grow strawberries, and it was soon time to harvest them. He had learned how to grow strawberries from Eliza Winn. He was able to collect money for his pledge by selling the harvested strawberries to local foreigners, explaining to them his reason for selling them. The new church building was quickly completed, and on July 19, 1891 a dedication ceremony was held. The Secretary General of Ishikawa Prefecture attended, as did the mayor of Kanazawa and other celebrities.

Rev. Winn sketched the layout of the building, and the architect Hattori drafted the site plan. The new building had a high gabled roof, and the décor was a simple Gothic style, with arched windows. The chapel area was also simply designed in the manner of a typical Protestant church hall, with the ceiling beams exposed and without a dropped ceiling. The combination of beams and tie bars was beautifully arranged, following the form of Victorian Gothic architecture. [1]

The old church organ had been destroyed with the collapse of the building. Fortunately, however, shortly after the former building had been completed, a new church organ had been ordered from the Mason Hamlin Co. in the United States. As a result, at the time of the collapse of the old building, a new organ had already been shipped. And so it happened that a new church organ was used in the dedication service for the new building. [2]

There were some people, however, who were not happy with the construction of the new building. The night of the dedication service, 50 to 60 people rushed towards the front garden of the church, with the intent to kill Pastor Banno. The pastor held a paper lantern high and cried out, "I am Kaichi Banno. You can kill me if you wish." With this he moved towards the mob, but as they were in an uproar in disarray, he was able to escape and somehow made his way home.

In 1892 the church hall was rebuilt, and with its construction there was renewed energy for the church's mission to spread the Christian faith. That year the church membership reached 178. Sunday School was resumed, but with more adults than children.

In August of that year a special commemorative service was held. Special guests who were invited included Kajinosuke Ibuka of Meiji Gakuin University, and Masahisa Uemura, leader of the Japan Christian Church. Many people gathered at the new church building to hear Jesus preaching the Gospel of Jesus Christ.

2. The Death of Ms. West

In November 1892 the Secretary of the World's Women's Temperance Union, Ms. Mary Allen West, came to Kanazawa from New York. She was a teacher at Knox College, and decided to see Eliza at her home in Japan. And so Ms. West made the long trip from New York to Kobe. From Kobe she travelled to Kanazawa, taking the usual path of train, rickshaw, a small steam ship, and a palanquin. Over the course of the journey, however, she became seriously ill, and upon reaching Kanazawa had to remain in bed. Eliza provided round the clock care for Ms. West, not getting any sleep herself. In spite of her efforts Ms. West passed away in Kanazawa. Thomas had asked the governor to send an American doctor from Kobe, but the request arrived too late. Three days after her death, temporary funeral [formal funeral by Ms. West's family to be held in the United States] was held for Ms. West at the new church. Representatives from the American Consulate arranged for her body to be sent back to the United States several days later.

The World's Woman's Christian Temperance Union was established in 1870 in the central United States as a Prohibition Movement. Eliza's father, Silas Willard's distant relative Frances Willard, founded this organization, which became a world wide union. This Christian women's organization continues to address social issues even to the present day.

3. A Crisis for the Independent Church with the Resignation of Pastor Banno

Pastor Banno became increasingly aware after becoming pastor of the Kanazawa Church that the weather there was unhealthy for him. He also experienced exhaustion from his hard work on the church building reconstruction. He submitted his letter of resignation to Rev. Winn, who was the chair of the Kanazawa Church Session. The Session accepted his intent to resign, and Pastor Banno transferred to a church in the city of Niigata in March 1893.

The Kanazawa Church was left without a pastor for one year and four months with Pastor Banno's departure. This situation is described in the book, The 110 Year History of the Kanazawa Church, (*Kanazawa Kyokai 110 nen shi*] with the following entry.

> We had trouble finding a new pastor. We had asked Tamisaburo Sugita who had studied at Doshisha University to be our temporary pastor. But due to a spirit of unrest in the church it was difficult to convince anyone to take the place of Pastor Banno. In an incident that proved to be critical for the life of the church, an influential elder in the church had been slandered, and there was dissension, which disrupted the church's sense of unity and spirit of service. This period of unrest became a great problem for Rev. Winn. In October 1894, Shinkichi Takagi became the pastor of the church. However this was

about the time of the beginning of the Sino-Japanese War, when the
7th Regiment based in Kanazawa became involved in the conflict.
With the beginning of the war, there was an increase in nationalistic pressure on thought, education and religion. The pressure in the
community on those who were Christian became more intense, with
an increase in the incidents of slander and suppressing the expression of their faith. Within the church, several elders and the secretary resigned. This trend led to a decline in the church's financial
management, so that part of the pastor's salary had to be paid from
the church's general fund. In this extraordinary situation, in March
1896 the congregation had to request financial assistance from the
Board of Foreign Missions in the United States. [(3)]

4. A Critical Incident

A "critical incident" was mentioned in the preceding section. Individuals from both within and outside the church slandered and
threatened Yutaro Mizuto, an elder in the Kanazawa Church. He had
been acting as a sincerely committed elder of the church since 1886.
In the community, he had contributed to the development of local in-
dustries, including transportation, heavy machinery, dairy farming,
and the raising of livestock. He was also very active in the political
life of the area, serving as President of the Kanazawa Chamber of
Commerce, a member of the Prefectural Diet, its legislative body, as
well as a member of the national House of Representatives. After his
death, it was recorded on the tombstone erected by volunteers, that
"He was great and decisive by nature, regarded righteousness as very
important, and all respected him." He was indeed this kind of person. [(4)]

But since he was a Christian at a time of strong nationalist senti-
ment, there were public attempts to kill him. In July 1893, there were
two slanderous letters to the editor that appeared in local newspa-
pers. Each tried to diminish his political stature and reduce the confidence of the people. The country was entering a period of time of
extreme nationalism and control of religious thought. The oppression

of Christianity was about to begin. Public behavior became more like that of a mob. People were becoming manipulated by ultra-nationalist propaganda.

The Christian community in Kanazawa began to experience the negative impact of this nationalistic fervor. The head of the Kanazawa Girls' School, Ikujiro Mizuashi, was involved in an incident that demonstrated the influence of extreme nationalism. On November 3, 1893, the Emperor's Birthday (or *Tencho-setsu*), he raised the Japanese flag during a school gathering and read the "Edict of Education." The "Mission" had been a standing committee which met regularly to make decisions on the operations and budgets of the "Stations" or mission projects. He was consequently advised by the "Mission" to resign his position. However he argued with Elder Mizuto on this directive. Ikujiro Mizuashi had graduated from Meiji Gakuin University and came to Kanazawa in 1892. He transferred his church membership to the Kanazawa Church, and in September 1893 became head of the Hokuriku Girls' School. The outcome of this incident was that Elder Mizuto resigned his position as elder and informed the church that he wished to transfer his membership to the Tonomachi Church. The church's third pastor, Shinkichi Takagi arrived in October 1894, and he soon tried to persuade Elder Mizuto to withdraw his resignation. Elder Mizuto was elected by the church as elder for the following year. He insisted on his resignation being accepted, however, and in February 1895 it was accepted. The new pastor, Shinkichi Takagi, was born in Shizuoka Prefecture. He had studied at Daigaku Nanko, which later became Tokyo University. While he was teaching English at the university he attended church, and heard a sermon by Masahisa Uemura. He decided to be baptized and accepted the Christian faith. He began to attend the Shitaya Church, where he was elected elder. As a member he was inspired by his new faith, became ordained, and in 1880 participated in a mission trip to other parts of Japan. He travelled to Chiba Prefecture, Ashikaga, and Mito, and spread the Gospel preaching on the streets of these communities. With the recommendation of Pastor Banno and Masahisa Uemura, he became pastor of the Kanazawa Church.

5. Aftereffects of the incident

There were many elders and deacons who began to express their desire to resign from the church. Over the course of several General Assemblies, however, Pastor Takagi worked to persuade them to remain, and avoid a worsening of the church's situation. The church's status as an independent congregation deteriorated as reports of the incident spread. Reports of this event affected the congregation for many years. The financial condition of the church began to deteriorate.

One of the early members of the Kanazawa Church, Daigen Nishimura, who had been baptized by Rev. Winn, told him that he would like to withdraw his membership as a result of the incident. His desire to withdraw his membership was in response to the reluctance of the "Mission" committee to provide financial assistance to the church despite the seriousness of their financial crisis. His concern may also have been tied to the fact that between one-fourth and one-third of the church's monthly income had been provided by the financial support of the Women's Missionary assistance, as well as the personal support of Rev. and Mrs. Winn. In his conversations with Rev. Winn, Daigen Nishimura asked that the plate offering be doubled to help meet the expenses of the church. The women missionaries that were mentioned in his conversations with Rev. Winn were Laura Naylar Thomson and Kate Shaw. They had helped Mary Hesser during her illness, and had been assigned to teach at the Kanazawa Girls' School by the Chicago chapter of the Woman's Presbyterian Board of Missions. They had graduated from the same school as Mary Hesser, Western Female Seminary. They worked with Mary Hesser at the Kanazawa Church and the Sunday School of the Tonomachi Church, and attended services there. They both got along well with women members of the church as well as with Eliza Winn.

In October 1895, an Emergency General Assembly was held, and the proposal to donate 3 yen from Pastor Takagi's monthly salary was approved. The General Assembly of the Kanazawa Church was held in March 1896, and at that time it was decided to request aid from the Board of Foreign Missions of the Presbyterian Church in the United States. Rev. Winn completed the necessary procedures, so that from June 1896 the Kanazawa Church became a "Mission affiliated church," and was able to obtain subsidies for its budget.

Pastor Takagi had insisted on the Kanazawa Church being financially independent, so that when the church was approved for financial support, he said that he was willing to resign. The pastor had travelled around the Hokuriku district to promote his ideas of helping the Assembly Hall, and expanding the area of mission outreach, that the Kanazawa Church could survive independently. Pastor Takagi proposed that the Foreign Missions' subsidy would pay for the cost of mission outreach instead of funding the general budget. [5] The General Assembly of the church approved his proposal. Rev. Winn went immediately to renegotiate with the Mission, but the leadership of the Mission turned down this proposal.

Pastor Takagi was not satisfied with the outcome of these meetings, and as a result resigned his position and returned to Tokyo, giving as his reason for leaving an "unsuccessful mission."

6. A path to avoid hardship

Three years prior to the incident at Kanazawa Church, in 1890, Eliza Winn suggested that the recently baptized Keiji Yomota (who later changed his name to Keiji Nakamura) transfer his membership from the Kanazawa Church to the Tonomachi Church. There were two possible reasons for this suggestion. One was that the Tonomachi Church, established seven years prior, needed help in its mission outreach work. Rev. and Mrs. Winn were both concerned that the two churches, being separate entities in eastern and western parts of Kanazawa city, would compete with each other for members.

The other reason was that Eliza saw Keiji Yomota as a prospective preacher and wanted to give him a chance to be involved in church activities. Keiji became an elder of the Tonomachi Church in 1893, and decided to study at Meiji Gakuin University's Department of Theology. In 1902 he was ordained as a pastor for the rest of his career.

The Kanazawa and Tonomachi churches continued as affiliated organizations. When the incident occurred in 1897, the Kanazawa Church requested that the Tonomachi Church allow Kanji Mouri to be their joint pastor. This had been suggested by Mrs. Winn, so that both churches could continue to co-exist.

Chapter 20

The Women's Association, and Social Work

1. Leading activities of women members

Although the church was now facing a crisis, Eliza's faith remained firm. The words of the apostle Paul were engraved in her heart.

> But we have this treasure in earthen vessels, to show that the transcendent power belongs to God and not to us. We are afflicted in every way, but not crushed; perplexed, but not driven to despair; persecuted, but not forsaken; struck down, but not destroyed; always carrying in the body the death of Jesus, so that the life of Jesus may also be manifested in our bodies. (2 Corinthians 4:7-10)

Especially after Sunday services, Eliza Winn would enthusiastically lead the activities of the Church Women's Association. In so doing, she showed her desire to have women take part equally as church members, and also to let them have the experience of actual religious life. She most likely allowed Mary Hesser of Kanazawa Girls' School to assist in looking after the children.

The program for the Church Women's Association was as follows.

1. Mrs. Winn or someone who had studied under her would play the organ and sing hymns.

2. Women members would read the Gospel and Mrs. Winn would explain what had been read.

3. A few of the women would offer prayers.
4. The following events would follow:
   a. With help from the women members, make flyers for the services
   b. Pass out the flyers and tracts as well as send them by mail
   c. Learn to make "Oshie," raised cloth pictures
   d. Cook western style food together
   e. Bake bread and confectionaries
   f. Make ice cream
   g. Learn how to use a sewing machine
   h. Learn to do patching work
   i. Learn how to weave wool fabric
   j. Prepare for an all church bazaar
   k. Delivering clothes and food to the poor

2. The First Social Work in the Hokuriku District

The Hokuriku District suffered a severe famine in 1890. The price of rice rose so high that the general population suffered, and many people died. Kanazawa had become a municipality the year before the famine, but 5% of the population was below the poverty level. The prefectural government attempted to deal with this crisis, but was limited financially in what it could do.

Eliza could not allow this condition of extreme poverty to continue. She asked for assistance from three Protestant churches: the Kanazawa and Tonomachi Churches, and the newly founded Methodist Church.

Pastor Banno was elected as the chair of this project. Rev. Winn and other missionaries, as well as many church members enthusiastically participated in the project. Over 1500 people who had lived in poverty were saved from starvation. The total amount of the funds raised was 340 yen, of which 300 yen was collected from Rev. and Mrs. Winn, the other missionaries in the community, and from foreign mission societies. This rescue effort was the first example of social welfare work in the Hokuriku district.

The Women's Association of the church engaged in activities such as cooking western dishes, baking bread and confecitonaries, making ice cream, using the sewing machine, making patch works and weaving wool. These skills were taught to the local populace, who then turned these skills into a business. In this fashion, western culture and technology was introduced to the Hokuriku district. [1] Rev. Winn also contributed to this introduction of western culture and technology. These contributions included:

1) Teaching the technique of milking cows,
2) Making and repairing furniture such as tables and chairs,
3) Teaching how to paint,
4) The making of tin ware,
5) Making brushes,
6) Manufacturing tooth picks,
7) Teaching exercises using Indian clubs [a bowling pin shaped wooden clubs usually in pairs],
8) Taking apart and assembling bicycles.

3. Starting an orphanage

It was the winter of 1892. Rev. and Mrs. Winn were on their way home from a trip to town. They came across two or three children hunting for food in the garbage bins of private homes and stores. The snow was falling down from a gray sky. The children did not have umbrellas to protect themselves from the snow, and were running around in the snow enduring the falling temperatures. Eliza could not continue going home. She asked Thomas, "How can we help these children? I wonder if there would be a way that we could start an orphanage?" And so the operation of an orphanage began.

With the many social and economic changes that took place following the Meiji Restoration of 1868, there were many from the former warrior class who had lost their status and with it, their income. Many from this class had difficulty securing sufficient income for food and shelter. Children suffered the most. Hungry children wandered the streets wearing rags, but the prefectural government could not do anything.

Rev. and Mrs. Winn obtained the funding for an orphanage, and managed to open it near the church "Station" at Ishibiki-cho. Hungry children came one after another, and these children were filled with lice and were dirty. Mrs. Winn let the older girls' help, and cleaned the children one by one, providing them with clean clothes and feeding them every day. The original building chosen for the orphanage quickly became overcrowded, and so another building was selected that was close to the Winn's residence. This larger building was able to accommodate 40 to 50 more children. Fortunately there was a couple among the membership of the Kanazawa Church who wished to care for the orphans, so Mrs. Winn asked the couple to manage the facility. Mrs. Winn taught reading and writing Japanese, as well as the four fundamentals of mathematics: addition, subtraction, multiplication, and division. Rev. Winn taught the orphans how to make brushes and tooth picks.

Despite their efforts the orphanage had to be closed down after nine years. The first reason for the closure was that the husband of the couple in charge of the orphanage passed away. The second reason was financial: the Winns could not obtain ongoing financial support. Rev. Winn wrote a letter to the Board of Foreign Missions requesting financial assistance, and the request was denied. The reasoning of the Board was that running an orphanage deviated from their understanding of mission work. Eliza Winn wrote a letter in response to the Board's refusal, saying that the orphanage was not unnecessary work, and again requested financial assistance. However the Board did not change its decision, and the orphanage had to be closed. [2] [See the Appendix 2]

Chapter 21

The Establishment of Toyama Church and the Daishoji Assembly Hall

1. The Founding of the Sougawa Kogisho (Assembly Hall)

Over the course of their efforts to spread the Gospel message, Rev. Winn and others encountered persecution as well as obstacles placed in their path. Despite this resistance, they remained positive about their work. In May 1881, Rev. Winn and several Japanese elders held a mission gathering at Kanazawa's Kanaiwa Port. In that same year, Satoru Kato, the church secretary, Chuei Aoki, a divinity student, along with a church member, Daigen Nishimura, held gatherings in the cities of Nanao, Takaoka, and Isurugi. The two of them continued on in that same month to the cities of Mattou, Komatsu, and Daishoji. At all of these gatherings, without exception, the church members met resistance, but continued preaching regardless of the persecution.

Later on, Rev. Winn and other members of the Kanazawa Church went around the Hokuriku district, looking for a meeting place where a native Japanese preacher or assistant could stay and carry on mission work .

Cho Ishikawa, who had been baptized by Rev. Winn, offered his home in Toyama, and the first Christian service in the region was held there. A worship service was held at the Ishikawa's home in October 1881. Cho Ishikawa and Maki Nagao attended the service.

Maki Nagao's father Hachinomon Nagao was also present, and as an Elder of the Kanazawa Church provided the sermon for the worship service.

Maki Nagao had been studying under Rev. Winn at the Hokuriku Eiwa School's Seminary, but from April to December 1883 began to work as an apprentice preacher at the Hoshii-cho in Toyama City. The place he stayed was probably at Cho Ishikawa's house, and this probably was the beginning of the Sougawa Assembly Hall.

2. From Sougawa Assembly Hall to Toyama Assembly Hall

The revenue from the first crop of the season was dedicated to Christ at the Sougawa Assembly Hall. Other religious activities in the area included the baptism by Rev. Winn of Cho Ishikawa, his wife Sou, their son Hikaru and his wife Tatsu. The service was held at the Kanazawa Church in July 1883.

The following year, in April 1884, Maki Nagao became the chief minister of the Sougawa Assembly Hall, and began his work spreading the Christian message in the community. From August of that year through September 1885 Maki Nagao received help in preaching from Seikichi Hayashi in preaching based at the Sougawa Assembly Hall. Another year passed, and Seikichi Hayashi was selected as the head minister, and worked on mission work in Toyama Prefecture.

There are three records of Rev. Winn's involvement in mission work of the Sougawa Assembly Hall [that remain intact for us to examine today.] They are as follows:

1) The Weekly Gospel (In Japanese, *Fukuin Shuho*) May 16, 1890 reports as follows;

> Last month, on April 23rd, a Christian worship service was held at Chukyoin-nai's Shintomiza. Rev. Winn provided the sermon, assisted by Chuko Toda and Ginzo Shinohara, and those who attended were impressed.

2) The Weekly Gospel (*Fukuin Shuho*) of October 17, 1890, records:

In this area it is rare to see people from other countries, but last month Rev. Winn and a few others came from Kanazawa and visited our town on their way to Toyama, and preached sermons. Many came to hear them out of curiosity, but were impressed that the sermons were delivered in fluent Japanese. [2]

3) In the October 1890 record of the Presbytery of Naniwa (*Naniwa Chukai*), the Ecchu district mission report (*Dendo Keikyo*) it is stated that "In the summer of 1890, Rev. Winn and Rev. Fulton each led gatherings, and attracted large audiences." [3]

As a consequence of all these activities in April 1891, as the result of discussions with many new Christian believers, an Extraordinary Assembly of Naniwa Presbytery met and approved a "Petition establishing an Assembly Halls at Daishoji and Toyama separating from the Kanazawa Church." As a result of this decision, Tatsu Ishikawa and 18 other members of the Kanazawa Church left to form the Toyama Temporary Church. At that time there was another assembly hall, other than the Sougawa Assembly Hall, so the new hall was called the Toyama Assembly Hall.

3. The Toyama Assembly Hall and Pastor Keiji Nakamura

Keiji Nakamura (former family name Yomota) was named as the pastor of the Toyama Church. The pastor and church members were all new. They acquired land and erected a new church building in the middle of Toyama City's Sougawa District, and in September 1903 held a dedication ceremony for the new church. From that time forward the Toyama congregation witnessed to their Christian faith in the midst of the Kingdom of Buddhism, treading a thorny path. Because of their efforts, ten years later, in April 1912, the Naniwa Presbytery standing committee that had been established to support the Toyama Assembly Hall becoming the Toyama Church approved the building of the church. After thirty years of hardship, the prayers of Christians in Toyama were heard at last. They endured persecution, yet were able to construct the church. Rev. and Mrs. Winn were in mission work in Osaka at the time of this achievement, but were most happy to hear the news.

Keiji Nakamura first encountered Christianity at the Kanazawa Church in autumn of 1888. He attended worship services at the church, and also was able to hear Rev. Winn's lecture on Primary Questions and Answers" at the Hokuriku Eiwa School. He was baptized by Pastor Kaichi Banno. In 1893, while he was a dormitory superintendent for the Hokuriku Eiwa School, the dormitory burned down. Feeling responsible for this tragedy he resigned his position. At the advice of Mrs. Winn, he studied at the Divinity School at Meiji Gakuin University. After serving in the army during the Sino-Japanese War, he returned to the Kanazawa Church at the invitation of Rev. Winn. In 1902, he became the senior pastor of the Toyama Assembly Hall, a position he held for 17 years.

Pastor Nakamura's wife Nao was the first graduate of the Kanazawa Girls' School, and was a student under Mary Hesser. In 1887, Nao was baptized by Pastor Chuei Aoki. She spoke fluent English, was very sociable, and was a good intermediary between the foreign missionaries and the Japanese people. She was very passionate in her mission work, and often wrote letters to the members of the church, and visited their homes and provided encouragement.

4. The Daishoji Assembly Hall, and Maki and Matsue Nagao

Prior to these events, in August 1881, Rev. Winn, preacher Seikichi Hayashi as well as other members of the Kanazawa Church had travelled together to the cities of Matto, Komatsu, and Daishoji. Their purpose had been to hold mission outreach gatherings, and they encountered great difficulties, as has been mentioned previously.

Nearly ten years later, in April 1891, fifteen members of the Kanazawa Church left to help establish the Daishoji Assembly Hall. Their departure took place three months after the roof of the Kanazawa Church had collapsed from the weight of the heavy snow on the roof.

Then in April 1896, Maki Nagao took over the mission at the city of Daishoji, which turned out to be a demanding task. Although ostracized by the townspeople, he called on his family to move with him to Daishoji. With his family moved in, the local people decided to not sell anything to them. They had to ask Mrs. Winn to send them food and other necessities of living, and even with this support barely survived. Furthermore, their children were bullied at school.

The students at the Sunday School were all the children of pastors, and there were only a few people in attendance at the evening gatherings for adults. All this did not deter preacher Nagao, who delivered his sermon to the lampposts and the pillars.

Nagao moved with his family in 1901 to Tonomachi Church. His mission work at Daishoji had resulted in just a few people converting to Christianity. In 1907 he accepted a call to become pastor of the Toyohashi Church. It was there that he met Toyohiko Kagawa, who at the age of 19 became an apprentice preacher. Kagawa was at that time suffering from pulmonary tuberculosis. Nagao and his wife Matsue provided excellent care for him, and he began to recover from his illness. Later on, when Kagawa became famous as a great communicator and advocate for social welfare, he remembered those days with Nagao and his wife. He commented: "I thank God that this preacher appeared in Japan. A person like him should be called a saint." The most appropriate title for Maki Nagao would be "hidden saint but immersed in God." [4]

Nagao's wife Matsue was known as a loving person. She lived humbly and was kind to all she met. One winter evening, returning home from shopping, she heard a girl crying from a nearby house. Looking into the house, she saw a seven or eight-year-old girl being beaten probably by her mother with hot iron chopsticks. Matsue entered the house and set the girl free. The girl then clung on to Matsue, so she took her outside the house.

Inquiring among the neighborhood housewives, Matsue discovered that the girl had been adopted. She was not allowed to go to school, and was beaten daily. Matsue determined that the girl would probably die if the situation continued.

Matsue then negotiated with the mother of the girl to release her, paying her what was then a large sum of 5 yen to set her free. She then brought the girl to her own home, where she already had eight children of her own, so that altogether she now had nine children to care for.

Her husband Maki was later transferred from Daishoji to Tonomachi Church. Through all these years Matsue invited many desperate children into their home, and took good care of them. For Matsue, the orphanage that had been started by Mrs. Winn provided a good model for caring for large numbers of chidren.

There was at that time an orphanage called "Kanazawa Orphanage" (the present day Baiko-kai) in the city of Kanazawa. Many orphans attending the Elementary School would often visit the Nagao home. Rev. Daniel McKenzie founded the Kanazawa Orphanage. He first taught English at the Senior High School No. 4. He later became a missionary and Chair of the Division of Japan Methodist Churches of the Kanazawa District. Mrs. Winn's orphanage probably provided a good model for him at that time.

Chapter 22

The Hokuriku Eiwa School Forced to Close

1. The Hokuriku Eiwa School and its challenges

Rev. Porter was invited to Osaka in 1888, and so the management of the school was turned back over to Rev. Winn. He requested more funding from the Board of Foreign Missions of the Presbyterian Church in the United States, and with the donations he received the school was able to erect a temporary gymnasium. Eliza was very busy with her duties at the church but took the time to teach English, history, English songs, and ethics (Bible study in English.)

Thomas and Eliza encouraged the use of the English dictionary when they were teaching English. Webster's English Dictionary (revised 1847) was available at the Hokuriku Eiwa School for a long time. When their students had questions about English usage, they would often respond with "Go check Webster!"

Eliza also taught both the History of Christianity and Christian Ethics at the Divinity School at the Hokuriku Eiwa School (formerly the Aishin School). The class on the History of Christianity introduced to students the three great religions of the world [Islam, Buddhism, and Christianity]. In this class, Eliza made an effort to explain the differences between Catholicism and Protestantism. Her class on Christian Ethics was based on her understanding of a biblical basis for ethical development, giving lectures and seminars using both the

English and Japanese versions of the Bible.

The Hokuriku Eiwa Assembly Hall was built on the compound of the Hokuriku Eiwa School in 1890. The new Assembly Hall became the site for the preaching of sermons and mission outreach programs led by Rev. and Mrs. Winn, as well as women missionaries at the Kanazawa Girls' School and occasionally students from the Divinity School.

Two years later, in April 1892, an influenza epidemic swept through the school, and it was forced to close down for ten days. In June of that same year, Dr. Hepburn and Hideteru Yamamoto edited and published the Japanese language Dictionary of the Bible (*Seisho Jiten*). Rev. and Mrs. Winn began using this resource in their lectures and seminars.

This was also a time in the history of Japan when waves of "Imperial Nationalism" were very strong, and overwhelmed both the Christian churches and the Christian schools. The recent Imperial Constitution [1889] and the Educational Rescript [1890] shaped popular thinking and was the foundation for the building of the modern state. All religions including Christianity were permitted under the condition that they did not deny the duty of loyal citizens to regard the Emperor as God. [1] Spiritual conditions in Japan are well revealed in three documents from that period: the Educational Rescript of 1890; the Order of the Ministry of Education of 1891, which determined annual holidays and rituals; and the work by Tetsujiro Inoue, *The Collision of Education and Religion*, published in 1893 reflects well the waves of "Imperial Nationalism."

As was expected, in December 1893, the School received official word from the Prefecture that the use of the "Old and New Testaments" was prohibited. The use of the Bible as a resource was critical for the existence of a Christian school, and was the foundation for the Hokuriku Eiwa School and the Kanazawa Girls' School.

2. Rev. Winn's agony and prayer

Rev. Winn wrote a letter to the Board of Missions of the Presbyterian Church in the United States reporting on this situation, providing information on the spiritual hardships in Japan, and how the churches and schools were confronting this hardship.

> And now I will tell you of a new and serious problem which has come upon us. One week ago notification from the Government was sent to both the Boys' and Girls' Schools, that we cannot teach the Bible any longer in them! It is now absolutely prohibited either as a compulsory or optional study. We have had a couple of conferences among ourselves on the subject.... We foreign missionaries and Japanese Christians are a vent in the opinion that we can't give up the Bible... If religious liberty is granted by the Constitution the present decision of this Ken [Prefectural] Government will certainly be reversed.... It seems to me that this ought to be made a test case if need be so as to be a guide to us and everybody else in the future... The Contention or position of this Ken Government is that our schools are of the same grade as the Government Schools, in which the Government doesn't allow religious teaching and therefore we can't be allowed teaching the Bible in ours. But ours are not Government Schools.... In regard to sending any more laborers to Kanazawa, you see the position we are in and of course will postpone all action, until we know what we are to do about our schools. In the mean time, we want instructions from the Board as to what we shall do in case the Bible is prohibited. It seems to me that in case the present decision is not reversed we shall have to give up our schools. We can't give a Christian education to even the children of Christian families, much less can we train up young men and women by leading them to believe in Christianity through our schools....
> We daily commit the whole matter to the Lord and pray for help and guidance in it. This help and deliverance is our only hope.
> Pray for Japan in these times when the Evil One seems to be doing his best to thwart and over-turn the teaching of the Truth. [2]

Chapter 23

The Translation of *Life of John Paton*

1. Summary of *Life of John Paton*

Eliza's personal agony and prayers were the same as those of her husband Thomas. However, in the midst of their struggle, there was still work to be done. It was to abridge and translate into Japanese the autobiography of the Scottish missionary John Paton, *Missionary to the New Hebrides, an Autobiography.* It was translated into Japanese and published in 1889 with the help of Suenobu Sanno, an elder of the Kanazawa Church and head of the Kanazawa Girls' School.

The following provides a) a brief description of John Paton, b) a summary of the autobiography which Eliza translated, and a part of "Namakei's Sermon" is introduced.

a) John Gibson Paton (1824-1907) was born as the son of a poor merchant in Scotland's countryside. His parents were devout members of the Scotch Presbyterian Church. After graduating from elementary school, John Paton went to Glasgow to work on a farm. Completing studies of the Bible and theology from the pastor, John went back to his home town and taught at an elementary school, but was called by a local church to preach. Within his parish, one drunkard quit drinking and became an earnest believer, and in this manner the Gospel spread among the poor workers in Glasgow. After preaching for ten years, John Paton studied theology as well as medicine at the university. He was ordained as a missionary and sent to the New

John G. Paton

Hebrides in the Solomon Islands. John and his wife were the first missionaries to Anthenium Island as well as Tanna Island.

Living conditions at Tanna Island were not sanitary. John and his wife arrived at the island the following year, and his wife was going to give birth. However, both mother and baby died due to the unsanitary conditions. Later on, John himself came down with a high fever, from which he recovered. But many local people contracted the measles, and about one-third of the population died.

b) Life on Tanna Island was savage beyond the imagination. People worshipped idols, and priests would take away people's lives through the use of magical powers. They stole, killed each other, and ate the flesh from dead bodies. Women were just slaves to the men on the island, and there were no feelings of love among married couples. When a man died his widow was thrown into the sea, and old people would starve to death. Girls of poor families were killed when they were born, and men would kill their wives when they were unable to bear children.

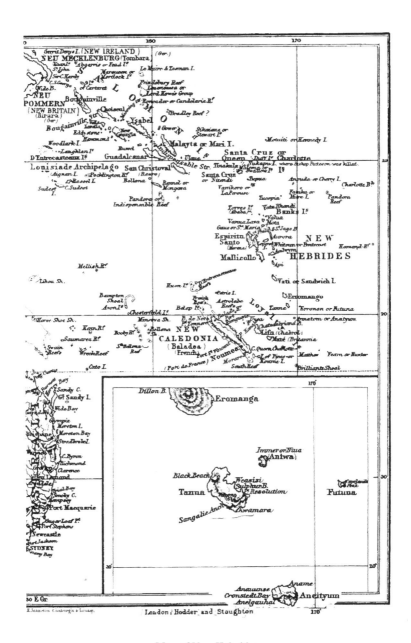

Map of New Hebrides

It was a difficult task to preach the Gospel to these people. But John Paton built a church, and led services and worship. He erected a school building, and translated parts of the Bible into the native language.

There were obstacles to the spread of Christianity. Things were stolen, people's lives were threatened, and John's house was set on fire. The persecution of Christians became increasingly severe. John Paton saw few other missionaries come to the island, and local people who had converted to Christianity were killed and became martyrs. John eventually was forced to leave the island.

John Paton decided that it was necessary for him to move to New South Wales, and five years later he returned to his home town. He then married a friend of his deceased wife, and returned to Tanna Island. In 1866 John began preaching in Aniwa Island. It was indeed a primitive place. He built an assembly hall, a school and an orphanage. He [arranged for] the care of children without parents, but accepted an unexpectedly large number of children, and had a hard time finding enough food for them.

People on the island continued to quarrel with each other, and even fought and killed each other. John believed that the true God of his faith forbids these kinds of acts, and preached that the Lord God had sent his only Son Jesus Christ to bring peace to God's people. The aging chief of the island people, and others who believed in this Christian God were baptized, but they suffered persecution from the people of their own tribe.

2. Namakei's oath of faith

Aniwa Island is a coral island. When people drank the rainwater, they became ill. [Rain water is safe to drink if drank immediately after the rainfall, but there is a problem of storing water]. Paton suggested that they dig a well to find water that was safe to drink. All of the people of Aniwa were against his suggestion. However he had some people dig a hole and rewarded them for their work, then he himself dug the hole deeper until he finally reached a source of underground water. He let people drink from this new well, and the islanders belatedly responded to the safe water with cries of joy.

A few days after the well was completed, Namakei asked Paton for permission to speak at the worship service the following Sabbath, and Paton accepted his request.

The worship service began on schedule as usual. Paton read from the Gospel, and then Namakei began speaking. Although there were a few who wanted to disrupt the service, Namakei continued to speak while holding on to his weapons. He gave his listeners the following message.

"Friends of Namakei, men and women and children of Aniwa, listen to my words! Since Missi [Rev. John Paton] came here he has talked many strange things, we could not understand—things all too wonderful; and we said regarding many of them that they must be lies. White people might believe such nonsense, but we said that the black fellow knew better than to receive it. But of all his wonderful stories, we thought the strangest was about sinking down through the earth to get rain! Then we said to each other, The man's head is turned; he's gone mad. But the Missi prayed on and wrought on, telling us that Jehovah God heard and saw, and that his God would give him rain. Was he mad? Has he not got the rain deep down in the earth? We mocked at him; but the water was there all the same. We have laughed at other things which the Missi told us, because we could not see them. But from this day I believe that all he tells us about his Jehovah God is true. Some day our eyes will see it. For today we have seen the rain from the earth."

Then rising to a climax, first the one foot and then the other making the broken coral on the floor fly behind like a warhorse pawing the ground, he cried with great eloquence:

"My people, the people of Aniwa, the world is turned upside down since the word of Jehovah came to this land! Whoever expected to see rain coming up through the earth? It has always come from the clouds! Wonderful is the work of this Jehovah God. No god of Aniwa ever answered prayers as the Missi's God has done. Friends of

Namakei, all the powers of the world could not have forced us to believe that rain could be given from the depths of the earth, if we had not seen it with our eyes, felt it and tasted it as we here do. Now, by the help of Jehovah God, the Missi brought that invisible rain to view, which we never before heard of or saw, and," —— (beating his hand on his breast, he exclaimed),——

"Something here in my heart tells me that the Jehovah God does exist, the Invisible One, whom we never heard of nor saw till the Missi brought Him to our knowledge. The coral has been removed, the land has been cleared away, and lo! the water rises. Invisible till this day, yet all the same it was there, though our eyes were too weak. So I, your Chief, do now firmly believe that when I die, when the bits of coral and the heaps of dust are removed which now blind my old eyes, I shall then see the Invisible Jehovah God with my soul, as Missi tells me, not less surely than I have seen the rain from the earth below. From this day, my people, I must worship the God who has opened for us the well, and who fills us with rain from below. The gods of Aniwa cannot hear, cannot help us, like the God of Missi. Henceforth I am a follower of Jehovah God. Let every man that thinks with me go now and fetch the idols of Aniwa the gods which our fathers feared, and cast them down at Missi's feet. Let us burn and bury and destroy these things of wood and stone, and let us be taught by the Missi how to serve the God who can hear, the Jehovah who gave us the well, and who will give us every other blessing, for He sent His Son Jesus to die for us and bring us to Heaven. This is what the Missi has been telling us every day since he landed on Aniwa. We laughed at him, but now we believe him. The Jehovah God has sent us rain from the earth. Why should He not also send us His Son from Heaven? Namakei stands up for Jehovah!" [1]

The aged Chief's talk was very influential with his people, and many were converted to the Christian faith. Eventually the entire island became Christian. They gave up their idols, and learned how to read and write at school, and worked earnestly. They established a church that listened to God's word, and celebrated the sacrament of communion. "The Commandments of Aniwa Island" were established according to the rules in the Bible as interpreted by the church, and evil deeds were punished according to these rules. And in the year of the famine, everyone helped each other, and in so doing overcame this disaster. The aged Chief Namakei continued to preach the Gospel, until a few years later when he passed away while preaching.

3. Special thoughts of Mrs. Winn on *Life of John Paton*

The year after she completed the translation of *Life of John Paton*, Eliza wrote a letter to the Board of Foreign Missions asking for financial aid for managing the orphanage. In this letter she mentioned the translation:

> I should perhaps confess that last year I took time with a native helper to translate into Japanese *Life of John Paton* but like the work in the Orphanage, it was done in addition, and not at the expense of time which should be devoted to missionary effort. I think I can truly say that I have never had opportunity to do more real missionary work, and it is the highest happiness I know, to teach the Bible to those who are eager to hear. [2]

Eliza's love for her work as a translator of *Life of John Paton* can be understood from this letter.

Chapter 24

The Death of Mary Hesser and the Winns' Furlough in the United States

1. Mourning of the Death of Mary Hesser

In late September 1894, a letter arrived from Los Angeles notifying the community of Mary Hesser's death. Three years after beginning her work at the Kanazawa Girls' School, Mary told the school officials that she could not recover from her feelings of numbness. The diagnosis that had been made by a physician was "catarrh." However it was obvious to everyone that the cause of her illness was stress and worries connected to her work, as well as the cold weather of Kanazawa.

Mary had returned to the United States briefly in September 1891 to recover from an illness. However when her condition improved she came back to Japan in April 1893 and returned to work. The following year, however, in January 1894, it was determined that the tumor had grown, and so in April she went back to the United States from Kanaiwa Port. The teachers and students of the Kanazawa Girls' School as well as her friends saw her off. It was a sad day for all those she left behind. Mary was treated at a hospital in Los Angeles, which had been introduced to her by a friend of Francina Porter of the Eiwa Kindergarten. But on September 1, 1894, Mary passed away. She was 41 years old. She had served all her life in Christian Education, and had acted as a woman missionary.

Eliza had trusted and respected Mary for the entire time that they had worked together. Mary had founded the Kanazawa Girls' School, and had done a wonderful job of managing its day to day operations. Thinking ahead of the future of the school, she worked to train those who would be her successors. She was a woman of the highest integrity. She loved children, and could be called a "true educator." Her faith was grounded in intellect, and she was not easily swayed by emotional appeals. She read the Bible well in both English and Japanese. The motto of the Kanazawa Girls' School (the present day Hokuriku Gakuin) was "The fear of the Lord is the beginning of wisdom." (Psalm 111:10)

Eliza had very strong feelings of affection for Mary Hesser. Eliza was saddened when she heard about the death of her friend, but she also recalled many memories of times that they had been together. She recalled singing a hymn at the opening of the Kanazawa Girls' School, and that Mary had delivered an impressive speech. Eliza remembered when Naylar Thomson became ill with typhoid fever, and was nursed back to health by Mary over a period of two months. Eliza also remembered when Mary herself became ill and had to be absent from her work, and how Eliza had temporarily taught her classes. And she also recalled how Mary would take care of Eliza's own children when she had to lead activities for the women of the church.

On October 1, 1894 the Kanazawa Girls' School held a special memorial service in Mary Hesser's honor on a special holiday set aside for the occasion. Suenobu Sanno, the head of the school, read Mary's personal history, and Rev. Winn paid tribute to her and gave a prayer. Eliza was of course in attendance for this service.

2. Furlough for Rev. and Mrs. Winn

On June 7, 1897, Rev. Thomas and Eliza Winn and their three children left Kanazawa for a one year furlough in the United States. They had not taken any time for a vacation since they had arrived in Japan 20 years ago in 1877, and had never even taken the regular sabbatical leave that was indicated in their contract with the mission board. Thomas had returned to the United States for about a year beginning in 1886, but this time away from Kanazawa was required for him to receive treatment for the cerebral hemorrhage of his eyes. On the day of their departure for their furlough, they started off at 4:30 a.m. by rickshaw. The Hokuriku Railroad only went as far as Fukui at that time, so they had to be there before sunset traveling by rickshaw all day. The Winns reached the port of Yokohama, near Tokyo, and were able to board a ship bound for San Francisco. From there they took the Transcontinental Railroad to Galesburg, Illinois, where Eliza's mother Cordelia known as "wife of prudence" lived. There were several expectations that the Winns had for their one year furlough. Most importantly, the Winns both had to get good rest, and recover their health from many years of service. They also had to prepare themselves physically for their return to working in Japan. For their last few years at Kanazawa they had worn themselves down both in body and spirit as they tried to cope with the problems of maintaining the independent Kanazawa Church.

Another self-imposed expectation involved a consideration of the future of the churches in the Kanazawa area. The Winns had accepted as a personal obligation a mission to help plan the future of the Kanazawa Church, as well as the other churches in the Hokuriku district. There were many at that time who thought that when the Winns left on furlough that this was the end of an era in Kanazawa. This is clearly stated in the book, One Hundred Ten Years of the Kanazawa Church (*Kanazawa Kyokai Hyakujyunenshi*). However, as the Winns were well aware, this period was actually the beginning of an ordeal for the churches to discover their own life of faith in God following 20 years of their struggle for independence as churches. [1]

A third issue that demanded the Winns attention was whether or not to continue the Hokuriku Eiwa School. There was a need to clearly identify the recent restrictions that had been placed on the school, and have an accurate sense of the cultural climate that was sweeping Japan at that moment in its history. Searching for a solution to this recent change in conditions, Rev. Winn requested the opinion of both Rev. Alexander and the Board of Foreign Missions of the Presbyterian Church in the United States, and corresponded with the Board of Foreign Missions.

3. Eliza's education of their children

Providing their children a chance to attend school in the United States was another important expectation that the Winns had for themselves during their furlough. For Eliza, the education of their children was extremely important. Their education at home while in Japan is described in the book, *Thomas Clay Winn, The Life of an American Missionary in Early Modern Japan.*

> Rev. and Mrs. Winn had four children: two boys and two girls. The eldest daughter Mary was born in Yokohama, but all the rest were born in Kanazawa. All the children later became missionaries when they grew up, but their parents took great care of them during their childhood. They let their children have a basic education at home until they left home to attend American colleges. Religious education at home was considered important—to pray, to give thanks and to read the Bible, to sing hymns and attend church services. These were daily routines. On Sunday the whole family attended church services, and after returning home their talk centered on discussions about religious topics…. Mrs. Winn was particularly keen in the education of her children and was strict in guiding their conduct. The children were not spoiled and she was sometimes severe.[2]

It was important to Eliza in developing her children's character that each child help with household chores. Eliza was very busy with her work at the school, but she did all the housework as well: cooking, cleaning, washing clothes, and putting things in order. Thomas also would help with these chores, and each child had their own assigned tasks, and would help her around the house. Beyond these chores, Eliza also wanted their children to develop their own interests, and she encouraged them to play at things that they enjoyed. Their second son George raised a calf in the family garden. He also built a train, with wooden rails and two or three wooden carts in which 2 children could ride. Also below the cliff and the bamboo bushes there was a pond and a little boat. Some of the students from the Hokuriku Eiwa School and the Kanazawa Girls' School enjoyed riding in the boat.

4. The Winn children attend schools in the United States

The Winns had three children at the time that they returned to the United States. Their second son George was 15 years old. Their second daughter Julia was 11, and their third son Merle was 7 years old. [Their first son Willard had died in 1879].

Their first daughter Mary had already returned to the United States the year before, and was a first year student at Knox College. She was staying with her grandmother, Mrs. Willard, known in town as "the Woman of Prudence."

Eliza had taught their children at home while they lived in Japan, but knew how important it was to allow her children to attend public school, and nourish the development of cooperation and independence with other children. She registered George to attend high school, and Julia to enter elementary school. [Merle also probably attended elementary school]. Classes started in September, and her school-age children were registered to attend the local school.

As school started in September, the Winn family moved to a new address, 501 East Losey Street, Galesburg, Illinois, the home where Eliza grew up.

While they were on furlough, Thomas and Eliza had an opportunity to discuss the future of the Hokuriku Eiwa School. They decided that the closure of the school was inevitable. Consequently they reported their decision to the Board of the Foreign Missions of the Presbyterian Church and the issue was finally resolved.

For the two of them it was now a time to rest and regain their strength. They could go for leisurely walks outside the city and out in the countryside. They would walk slowly along the road in view of the Illinois prairie. One evening as they were walking along, it was nearing sunset. The pastoral scene of Galesburg was spread out before them. A couple working on their farm were putting away their farm implements for the day, and would soon be going home. Watching this scene unfold in front of them, Thomas remembered when he was last in Galesburg, and a terrible experience he had almost dying from falling from a carriage. Eleven years had passed since that time. For her part, Eliza must have remembered the scene from Jean Millet's "The Gleaners" and "The Angelus" which she had seen in her high school textbooks. This experience had taken place just prior to her meeting Thomas, who was at the time impressed with the innocent and pious paintings.

Chapter 25
Evangelism in the Kansai area

1. Moving to Osaka

Rev. and Mrs. Winn returned to Kanazawa with their youngest
son Merle in September 1898. But soon after their arrival they were
transferred to Osaka.

Rev. Winn had written the Board of Foreign Missions of the Presbyterian Church in the United States on this matter after they reached
Osaka.

> You see from the heading of this letter [that our address has
> changed] and we have really moved away from Kanazawa, and the
> work of that region which we loved so well. It was a very hard thing
> for us to decide to do, but most of the Mission seemed to think it
> best, so that we didn't feel like going in opposition to their judge-
> ment. [1]

The three churches that Rev. and Mrs. Winn founded with all their
efforts were the Kanazawa Church, the Tonomachi Church, and the
Toyama Evangelical Church. Each church had unique problems, but
each was moving towards establishing its independence. Japanese
head pastors or chief ministers were providing leadership of preaching as well as membership care. Although the churches continued to
operate in adverse circumstances, there was a gradual expansion of
their presence in the community. Rev. John Gaskin Dunlop arrived at
the Kanazawa Foreign Mission Station after Rev. Winn left for Osa-

ka. As far as the Kanazawa Girls' School was concerned, the school followed a plan to make it a pioneer institution in the area for girls' education. This plan had been initiated by Mrs. Winn, and further developed by Mary Hesser and her successors.

One regret for both Rev. and Mrs. Winn was that the Hokuriku Eiwa School ceased to exist. The Ishikawa Prefectural School was established in 1886, following the guidelines set up in the "Edict of Junior High Schools." In that year four junior high schools were founded, with 800 students in all attending. Also, any hope of continuing the Hokuriku Eiwa School was severely damaged by the extremely nationalistic mood of that era.

Following the direction of the Board of Foreign Missions of the Presbyterian Church in the United States, Rev. Winn sold the school land and building. He then went through the procedures necessary to close down the school [completing in September 1898].

In October 1898, only a month after their return to Kanazawa, Rev. and Mrs. Winn said farewell to each person who came to see them off, and left Kanazawa. By this time, the Hokuriku Railroad line had been completed, making the journey much easier than in previous years.

Rev. and Mrs. Winn had been involved in evangelical work in the Hokuriku District for exactly 19 years. Rev. Thomas Alexander was probably the one who had invited them to work in Osaka. He had been a good friend of Rev. Winn, and had arrived in Japan on the same ship. Where the Winns had served churches in the northern provinces, Rev. Alexander was in charge of expanding the activities of the Japanese Christian Church in the central Kansai district, the Sanyo district, as well as the southern districts in Shikoku and Kyushu.

With the help of three women missionaries, Rev. Thomas Alexander began his mission work at the northern Osaka Kita Church, as well as the Osaka Minami Church in the southern part of the city. One of the three women was Anne Garwin, who had studied at the same school attended by Mary Hesser, Western Female Seminary.

The three-year mission work of Rev. Alexander led to the founding of the Japan Christian Osaka North Union Church, the Japan Christian Osaka South Union Church, and the Union Girls' School (Osaka Women's School).

2. Evangelism in the Kansai District

The following account of the mission work of Rev. and Mrs. Winn is to be found in The Fifty Year History of the Japan Christian Osaka Minami Church. (*Nihon Kirisuto Osaka Minami Kyokai 50 nen shi*)

> Rev. and Mrs. Winn had helped our church at Kyobori for one year. Furthermore they moved to the Foreign Concession in Kawaguchi, and until 1906 worked in Sakai and other meeting places. They spread the Gospel message in the region, and for eight years helped our neighboring Osaka North and East Churches, as well as the Sakai Assembly Hall. Besides this they worked hard for the YMCA, the Sunday Schools, and Women's Groups. [2]

Rev. and Mrs. Winn were actively involved in supporting the evangelistic work of Rev. Alexander, and were always present when there was a church service. They would stand in front of the chapel for 30 minutes prior to the service, and welcomed members of the congregation with a cheerful greeting.

Besides giving sermons at the weekly services, Rev. Winn taught English classes. Eliza Winn read English books with youth members of the church, and led them in singing hymns. At the Sunday School, she read Bible stories to the children. She also organized the women members into a Woman's Society and studied community concerns, and worked on projects. Their oldest daughter Mary would come to their home in Japan for summer vacation from college. She loved her mother and respected her, and understood her mission work, helping with Sunday School and Bible Reading. [During summer vacation from June to August, it took Mary about 20 days one way and stayed with her parents in Osaka for several weeks.]

Eliza would often visit the homes of church members, and those who had expressed an interest in the Christian faith. She would get on a train, ride a bicycle, as well as walk, and would sometimes make her visits with church elders.

One day she left home for her usual visits, but did not return until 7:00 or 8:00 o'clock in the evening. Her family members were worried, and asked the police to search for her. She finally returned about 9:00 o'clock. She had traveled to Ibaraki, 20 kilometers (12 miles) away, to visit a church member. Once she arrived there, however, she discovered that there were few trains that would get her home, and consequently she got back quite late. She had traveled alone to Ibaraki City and called on people she encountered there to come to the church in Osaka.

The Winns also had regular gatherings in the town of Sakai, at the Assembly Hall, or *Kogisho*, which initially was the central part of their mission work. Sakai was located 16 kilometers (10 miles) from Osaka, and they would hold meetings there every weekday at the same time regardless of the weather. They would travel back and forth to Sakai on their bicycles. Eventually the Sakai Assembly Hall began to carry on its own activities, besides those provided by the Winns.

3. Tsutomu Miyoshi becomes a pastor

There is a special story that needs to be told here, about how Rev. and Mrs. Winn led Tsutomu Miyoshi into the Christian faith. Tsutomu Miyoshi had been a policeman. He had heard that Rev. Winn was a man of high morals, and out of curiosity came to attend the worship service. There he heard a Christian sermon for the first time in his life. Following his attendance at the service, Rev. and Mrs. Winn went several times to the police station where Miyoshi worked, and spoke with him on how to live a life of Christian faith and about the Gospel of Jesus Christ. Tsutomu Miyoshi was intrigued by Rev.

Winn's passionate preaching and the Winn's noble character, and decided to be baptized and become a Christian. He subsequently began seminar study at the Theological School of Meiji Gakuin. The respected theology teacher Masahisa Uemura had been teaching there, but abruptly moved to teach at Tokyo Theological School shortly after Tsutomu began his studies. Tsutomu Miyoshi consequently quit his studies at Meiji Gakuin. He began working for churches in Fukui and Takatsuki, but later on moved first to Manchuria and then to the United States at the invitation of Rev. Winn. He studied at Princeton University Divinity School for four years, and then from 1913 to 1928 was pastor of the Dalian Christian Church in Manchuria. Rev. Winn had invited Tsutomu to the Dalian Christian Church to provide ministerial support, as well as to help spread the Gospel in Manchuria.

One of Tsutomu's goals during his 15-year stay in Dalian was to build a memorial church in honor of Mrs. Winn. Pastor Miyoshi's dream came true with the building of the Shahekou Church in memory of Mrs. Winn.

After leaving Manchuria, Miyoshi became pastor of the Fujimicho Church in Tokyo led by Masahisa Uemura, presiding there for 23 years as pastor. He has written a preface for a book about Rev. Winn, Disciple of Japan; the Life of Thomas C. Winn (*Nihon no Shito: Thomas Winn Den*) 4th edition, by Shoshichi Nakazawa. All of Miyoshi's books were donated to Hokuriku Gakuin through Tetsuo Banjo, then President of Hokuriku Gakuin. The books are now held by the Hokuriku Gakuin's Mary Hesser Memorial Library. Tsutomu Miyoshi and Tetsuo Banjo were closely affiliated, as they had known each other through Rev. Winn.

Chapter 26
Evangelism in Manchuria

1. The Decision to go to Manchuria

Japan declared war against Russia on February 8, 1904 over territorial issues centered on Korea and Manchuria. The Japanese forces at first faced challenging battles against Russian forces. Having the financial support of both the United States and England, the Japanese military was able to maintain superiority over Russian forces at the Battle or Fengtian, and the Battle of the Japan Sea. The conflict soon reached the limits of either nation's ability to continue, and was ended with the signing of the Treaty of Portsmouth, on September 5, 1905, facilitated by US President Theodore Roosevelt. Kanzo Uchimura of "Mukyokai" Christian Church [Church for those not belonging to any particular church] persisted in his anti-war position for the duration of the conflict.

Masahisa Uemura (1858-1925), a leader of the Japan Christian Church, deserves mention at this point. The present day Yokohama Kaigan Church, which is part of the Church of Christ in Japan, have their roots in the early work of the Japanese Presbyterian Church, which in turn was influenced by the American missionary Dr. James Hepburn, as well as the missionaries from the Dutch Reformed Church, Rev. Samuel Brown and James Ballagh. With the ending of the war, the Japan Christian Church established its Evangelism Division, and Masahisa Uemura was made chair of the Board. Uemura was born as a samurai in the old hierarchy of the Tokugawa feudal system. He studied at the school founded by Samuel Brown, was also influenced by James Ballagh, and was converted to the Christian faith. He studied at the Tokyo Union Theological School, founded the Tokyo Ichibancho Union Church (now the Fujimicho Church) and was a pastor through his entire career. During this early period in his career, he taught at Meiji Gakuin University, established the Tokyo Theological School to educate and train new pastors, and attempted to liberate theological studies in Japan from the influence of the Board of Foreign Missions. He also published a magazine, News of the Gospel (*Fukuin Shimpo*), and tried to articulate the position of the Japanese churches. He thought of the Gospel as the foundation for the church, and contributed to the formation of the Japanese church and its theology.

As Board Chair of the Evangelism Division of the Japan Christian Church, Uemura wanted to take steps to begin evangelism in Manchuria at the end of the Russo-Japanese War. The Evangelism Division sent Secretary Kojiro Kiyama in December 1905 to three cities Lushun, Inkow, and Dalian. The Civil Affairs Chief of Dalian said that if the Japanese people were allowed unrestricted travel in Manchuria, then many Japanese citizens would come with their families. He also said, "We wish to extend an invitation to a well educated western missionary who would be able to teach not only the Bible, but also the English language, as well as cooking and sewing for Japanese housewives who tend to stay at home. If there are misunderstandings among foreigners residing in Manchuria, we hope that this western missionary would be able to explain the Japanese situation. We really wish such a missionary to be sent." [1]

Upon receiving the request from the Civil Affairs Chief of Dalian, Chairman Uemura consulted with Secretary Kiyama, and immediately sent a telegram to Rev. John Dunlop, who was at that moment in Manchuria on a visit to console victims of the Russo-Japanese War. His intention was to return shortly thereafter to the United States, so he turned down the offer to move to Manchuria. However he recommended that Rev. Winn, who was by then living in Osaka, to go in his place. Secretary Kiyama immediately went to Kawaguchi, Osaka, to visit Rev. and Mrs. Winn to explain the current situation in Manchuria to them. He shared with them his concern for the future of Manchuria, and asked for their help in evangelism there. The expectation that Secretary Kiyama outlined included supporting the Dalian Church, as well as evangelistic work in the area along the South Manchurian Railroad. That evening Rev. and Mrs. Winn prayed to the Lord for guidance, and the following morning accepted the offer, saying, "We believe that this is God's Will."

2. Arriving at Dalian

Their visas allowing them to travel to Manchuria were finally issued in August. The president of the Osaka Merchandise Vessel Company happened to be studying English from Rev. and Mrs. Winn, and so offered special assistance to them in their transition. The Director of Civil Affairs offered a house for them to use rent free for a year.

Rev. and Mrs. Winn arrived in Dalian in September 1906. They were the first foreign missionaries to enter the Japanese territory of Manchuria. A high ranking officer, Nobusuke Hibiki, greeted them upon their arrival.

It is appropriate to introduce Nobusuke Hibiki at this point. He was from Wakayama Prefecture in southern Japan, and graduated from the Japan Military Academy and the Military Administration Academy. He was promoted from Assistant Superintendent to Major General. While stationed in Tokyo, he became acquainted with Pastor Masahisa Uemura, and under his influence became a Christian. He was among the twenty-five Christians who in 1898 transferred from the Nagoya Church to the Kanazawa and Tonomachi Churches. He was elected an elder of the Kanazawa Church, but had to move to Sapporo in northern Japan in 1899. Later in his career he was able to help the Japan Christian Church's evangelism outreach in Taiwan. He was assigned to Manchuria in 1904, and held small Christian gatherings for soldiers and army civilian employees in Dalian and Yingkou. This marked the beginning of the Manchurian Mission. Later on, he went on to found the Tianjin Elementary School in China, and the Dalian Commercial School in Manchuria. Besides his work as a military professional, he put a lot of his energy into evangelism over the course of his life, and in 1933 established the Manchurian Mission and the East Aian Mission.

Rev. and Mrs. Winn initiated a meeting with Nobusuke Hibiki and Tsutomu Miyoshi, who had been pastor at the Takatsuki Church. With their help they devised and began to implement a precise plan for evangelism in the area.

The Gospel message resonated with the souls of the people. This attraction led to a gradual increase in attendance, at the Dalian Japan Christian Church, (later known as the Dalian Church) to where Sunday services attracted over 100 people. Rev. Winn would pass on his interpretation of the Bible. Mrs. Winn organized the Women's Association of the church, and provided instruction to them. Sometimes Rev. and Mrs. Winn would board the trains of the Manchurian Railroad, and preach to the people who lived along the railroad line. On those occasions, Tsutomu Miyoshi would always accompany them and he provided assistance.

3. The Construction of a Church Building, and the Flourishing of the Church

The construction of a church building was proposed at the Session of the Dalian Church, and was then later approved at the General Annual Meeting. The Manchurian government at that time provided a grant that supported part of the building fund, as well as set aside a piece of land in a great location at Xiguangchang in Dalian City. Donations to support the building fund came from the Dalian Church as well as from all over Japan. "Nobusuke Hibiki helped lay the groundwork for the building project, and Rev. and Mrs. Winn were directly involved in the construction phase. A tremendous amount of labor was put into the building, and as a result the Dalian Church nominated Rev. Winn to be their "Honorary Pastor." [2]

Actual construction of the building began in the autumn of 1906, and was completed in July 1907, with a ceremony of completion held the following December. The church building was big and magnificent, built with red bricks, with a tall steeple reaching high into the sky of Xiguangchang. With the new building completed, Rev. Winn and all the church members were excited to begin their evangelism work in earnest. Furthermore, the numbers of people attending the various gatherings of the church increased significantly. Facilities operated by Christians, such as the" Jikei" Hospital, the Commercial School, and the Women's Relief Center received the full support of the local community. There was a great expansion of social welfare programs in Dalian due greatly to the support of Christians. Local citizens appreciated and supported the activities of groups endorsing prohibition, as well as the development of youth groups, women's associations and self-help groups.

It was at this time that Rev. Winn received the title of Doctor of Divinity from his alma mater, Union Theological Seminary. [3]

4. Disputes within the Dalian Church

The Dalian Church entered a period where it was enjoying some success in the community. The church became known in the city as the "Xiguangchang Church," and was very familiar to the people. In 1910 a full time pastor was needed, and Misaku Miyagawa arrived to provide leadership. Rev. and Mrs. Winn thought that the timing was right to allow Pastor Miyagawa to take charge of the church, while they shifted their concentration to evangelism in cities located along the Manchurian Railroad.

However a dispute soon arose within the church. Church members felt that there was a marked difference between the Christian theology of Rev. Winn and that of Pastor Miyagawa. Rev. Winn based his preaching on mystical spiritual experiences, whereas Pastor Miyagawa's concept of Christian belief was based on rational intellect and common sense. Pastor Miyagawa's theology was more with the current thinking of what was called the New Theology. His theological framework was more intellectual than emotional or mystical, and regarded the other style of thinking as an invalid belief system. [4] The situation of the Dalian Church was described in the following manner in *Thomas Clay Winn—The Life of an American Missionary in Early Modern Japan.*

> Some of those who were influenced by Rev. Winn had worried that the church would face a critical state, as their beliefs would be shaken to their foundations. These individuals called for a change in pastors. However there were those who defended Pastor Miyagawa and the church was split in two…. Although there were differences in Christian theology between the two leaders, there were many members of the church who admired Rev. and Mrs. Winn. For these people the root of the problem seemed to be found more in personal feelings than in a way of thinking. Rev. Winn was a man of character, and the noble manner of Mrs. Winn won the respect and love of many church members. [5]

Rev. and Mrs. Winn were most dismayed at this situation. They called on God in prayer to help. Each of them tried to get the two parties to compromise, but without success. Eventually the church conflict was reported in a newspaper.

As mentioned previously, there had been an instance at the Kanazawa Church where a critic of one of the church elders reported his opinion in the newspaper, and this had led to a setback in the church's goal of independence. In the later experience of the Dalian Church, the conflict was elevated to the level at which a new pastor's religious beliefs were questioned in a newspaper.

Mrs. Winn suspected that their presence contributed at least in part to the dispute. She discussed her concerns with her husband, and they made the decision to move away from Dalian and carry on their evangelistic work in the inner part of Manchuria.

Rev. and Mrs. Winn left Dalian in early October 1912. As a consequence of their departure, the elders and the secretary of the Dalian Church resigned at the same time. Hearing of their decision, Rev. Miyagawa resigned as well, and the church was without a pastor for a while. Members of the church who had supported Rev. Miyagawa left at that time, and formed a congregation of a different denomination. There were also those who joined the Anglican Church. After some time had passed, the Dalian Church invited Rev. Yakichi Sasakura of Yokohama Kaigan Church to be their pastor. The church also invited Tsutomu Miyoshi, who had just graduated from Princeton University Divinity School, to be successor of Pastor Sasakura. The church adopted the new name of the Evangelical Dalian Church.

5. A small house

Rev. and Mrs. Winn went on a mission trip through the cities between Dalian and Changchun, but had trouble finding a place to stay during their journeys. Somehow this problem was eventually solved. A wealthy merchant hosted them when they went to Yingkou. They stayed free at the Manchurian Railroad's Club Hotel when they visited Fushun. And they stayed at the house owned by the Mitsui Bussan Company as well as the house of a missionary from Scotland when they stopped at Fengtian (present day Shenyang).

Over the course of their travels, Rev. and Mrs. Winn continued to look for a semi-permanent place to stay. The Manchurian Railroad Company offered dormitory housing at Qianjinzhai for them to use. On October 7, 1912, they moved into their house. It had a 6 mat, 4 ½ mat, and 3 mat rooms (1 mat equals approximately 5.6ft x2.7ft) . Eight houses were joined together, and were poorly built. Seeing this development, Mrs. Winn said to those around her in a low voice:

> I came to Japan and moved from Yokohama to Kanazawa, then from

Kanazawa to Osaka. I lived in a smaller house each time. Transferring from Osaka to Dalian, I moved into an even smaller house. But now I have to live in a much smaller one. Probably the next time I move, I will be living in a small box. [6]

Those who later recalled her saying this jokingly could not believe it, for they realized that her prediction soon became a reality.

Chapter 27
Remembering Eliza

1. Eliza's death

Eliza's death came suddenly. She awoke as usual on October 8, 1912, at 6:00 o'clock in the morning, and went to the kitchen to prepare breakfast. She and her husband were planning to go to Fengtian to see a lady who was scheduled for surgery on her stomach, and were planning on returning home very late.

Her husband awoke and took time in their bedroom for his usual morning prayers. Suddenly he heard a strange sound, and puzzled listened carefully for further noise. He did not hear any sounds of movement from Eliza, so he called her name and went out to the kitchen. There he found her lying on the floor. Thomas was usually very calm in any situation, but he suddenly became very alarmed. He ran to her and tried to wake her, but found that she has stopped breathing. He ran outside and told his neighbor, the preacher Mr. Kawakami, that there was an emergency. Mr. Kawakami had someone run over to the Manchurian Railroad Company's hospital, and the doctor came right over. It soon became apparent that Eliza had collapsed from a cerebral hemorrhage, so that no treatment was possible. Thomas could not do anything more, and knelt down by her body and prayed that her soul be returned to heaven.

2. Eliza's funeral

Her funeral was held as a grand official church funeral of the Dalian Church. More than 500 people attended her funeral, which was held on October 12. Eliza and Thomas' son George, who was a pastor in Korea, attended with his wife, and his sister Julia and her husband. Also in attendance was Pastor Masaki Nakayama of the Fengtian Church.

The church was packed full, with many standing outside the chapel. After the solemn introit of the organ, the people in attendance sang a traditional hymn, *When I survey the wondrous cross,* one of Eliza's favorites:

> When I survey the wondrous cross
> On which the Prince of Glory died,
> My richest gain I count but loss,
> And pour contempt on all my pride.

The elder presiding at the service then read Psalm 90, one of Eliza's favorites.

> Lord, thou hast been our dwelling place in all generations.
> Before the mountains were brought forth,
> or ever thou hadst formed the earth and the world,
> from everlasting to everlasting thou art God.
> Thou turnest man back to the dust, and sayest,
> "Turn back, O children of men!"
> For a thousand years in thy sight are but as yesterday when it is past,
> or as a watch in the night.
> Thou dost sweep man away; they are like a dream,
> like grass which is renewed in the morning
> …Let thy work be manifest to thy servants,
> and thy glorious power to their children.
> Let the favour of the Lord our God be upon us,
> and establish thou the work of our hands upon us,
> yea, the work of our hands establish thou it.

The presiding elder then delivered a sorrowful prayer, and the congregation sang a hymn to consecrate her burial. The previous pastor of the church, Rev. Miyagawa, then read a life history of Mrs. Winn. A visiting missionary named Brian gave a sermon. He made reference to the words of a British noble, saying that he had felt welcomed when he toured Manchuria, but that the kindness of Mrs. Winn had been greater than even that experience.

Pastor Kawakami led the congregation in a prayer, which was followed by another of Mrs. Winn's favorite hymns, *Jesus, Thy Name I love*:

> Jesus, Thy Name I love,
> All other thoughts above,
> Jesus, my Lord!
> Oh, Thou art all to me!
> Nothing to please I see,
> Nothing apart from Thee,
> Jesus, my Lord!

Ten individuals then provided condolences to the family, and telegrams were then read which provided further condolences. Following these readings, the congregation sang another familiar hymn, *It is Well with My Soul*.

> When peace like a river attendeth my way,
> When sorrows like sea billows roll;
> Whatever my lot,
> Thou hast taught me to say,
>   "It is well with my soul,
>   It is well with my soul,
>   It is well, it is well, with my soul."

Rev. Winn then concluded the service with a message on behalf of his family, and led in the singing of the doxology. [1]

Grave of Eliza Winn

3. The erection of a gravestone and the publication of *The Life of Mrs. Winn*

The Dalian Church and the Women's Association immediately began planning to erect a gravestone for Mrs Winn's tomb, and publish a book, *The Life of Mrs. Winn*. After their plans were announced, donations arrived from all over Japan, so that enough was raised for them to accomplish their goals. The gravestone for Mrs. Winn was built and erected at Xiwangjiatung. The tomb itself was surrounded with a low granite fence. The tombstone was made of marble. Her children designed the cross on it, with the words "Tomb of Mrs. Winn" inscribed on it.

The ceremony commemorating the completion of the headstone was held in May 1913. Flowers were arranged on both sides of the tomb. There were about 250 people in attendance at the ceremony. Gumpei Yamamuro of the Salvation Army was among those who provided a eulogy for the occasion.

Hakuyo Shibata, who was the first person at the Dalian Church to be baptized by Rev. Winn, wrote Mrs. Winn's biography. *The Life of Mrs. Winn* was published in May 1913. [2]

4. Memories of Mrs. Winn

A later publication, Disciple of Japan: The Life of Thomas Winn (*Nihon no Shito: Thomas Winn Den)* was based in part on the memories of Mrs. Winn recorded in *The Life of Mrs. Winn*. The following excerpt is an example.

> Rev. Winn had a devout faith and a peaceful demeanor, and Mrs. Winn possessed a great faith and a deep sympathy for others. They had a harmonious relationship, and had a happy family.
>
> What astonished most people was how busy she was with her activities, active every minute. Her activities outside the home were centered on her Christian mission work. As a result, she was busy not only with her family, but with children's education, interacting with students and young people, as well as active in the Women's Association. Spreading the word of her Christian faith was her mission and her way of life….
>
> Mrs. Winn was faithful, obedient, reserved and warm hearted in her character. Her appearance was simple yet graceful, like a lily of the valley. She spoke kindly to others, and her behavior was gentle, perfect in action. She was truly a lovable woman. She was a good wife and a great mother, and her family was happy. Her family had the aura of a warm calm spring day.
>
> Mrs. Winn was often seen riding a bicycle. She would ride a bicycle on her visits to homes to spread the Good News, without showing any sign of fatigue, even though she was by then at a good old age. She would ride her bicycle for visits even in burning hot weather (more than 40 degrees C), or shivering cold (minus 30 degrees C). She was mentally and physically sound, and remained very active. She was never ill. She worked towards her goal of spreading the gospel message even in rainy and foggy of Kanazawa, or snowy and windy Manchuria.

Mrs. Winn always took yarn and knitting needles along with her wherever she went, even on her mission trips. While other people were sleeping on the sofa, Eliza would pull out her wool yarn and knitting needles and begin knitting socks or gloves. She would present them as souvenirs at the places where she visited. She was able to remember the houses where there were children, and would present these children with gloves or socks. It was one of things that she enjoyed doing.

Even if she had time to relax, she was always doing something. She would often listen to her husband when he was talking about a book that he was reading, but she was always knitting at the same time. When her hands were free they would be used for something; when her eyes were resting, they were still attentive. Her hands and eyes were always in motion. Even when Eliza was living in Osaka and was busy teaching English grammar and conversation to young men, she never stopped knitting or using her sewing machine.

Eliza prayed all the time. She had a firm belief that any problems in the world could be solved through prayer. So she would start the day with prayer when she got up in the morning, and when she had meals she would pray, and in the evening when she went to sleep she prayed. She preferred to be away from other people when she prayed. In the morning she would pray wherever she was when she awoke, but in the evening she prayed alone in an empty room.

Eliza was always enthusiastic in sharing her faith. One example of this was when she once invited a fish vendor into their home. She bought a piece of fish, but then she also talked about her faith and began a mission outreach to the fish vendors.... [3]

5. Rev. Winn following his wife's death

Rev Winn would write later in his memoir:

As my beloved wife passed away, my future seemed so dark, and it was not possible to stay in Manchuria. But as the Lord has ordered me to stay here, I have continued to stay for 1 or 2 years. I had wished to stay in Manchuria and for as long as possible. I hoped to work with members of various churches.[4]

Rev. Winn was gradually getting older, and could feel changes in his physical condition which affected his ability to manage his daily activities. Someone who was concerned about him suggested that he remarry, and he finally agreed to marry Miss Florence Bigelow, a teacher at the Shimonoseki Baiko Jogakuin (Girls' School).

Rev. Winn continued in his mission work in Manchuria , retiring in 1923, and he was 72 years old at that time. He and his wife Florence returned to the United States for a while. But his wife was invited to return as a teacher at the Hokuriku Girls' School, so they returned to Kanazawa. Rev. Winn helped with preaching at the Kanazawa and Tonomachi Churches which he had founded. But on Sunday, February 8, 1931 he passed away while preparing to preach a sermon. He was 79 years old.

Rev. Winn's oldest daughter Mary graduated from Knox College, and got married and had three children. She was living in Philadelphia with her family when she was diagnosed with cancer. She had surgery, but passed away after surgery and course of treatment lasting one and a half years. She left a message to her family and friends: "To the youth of our cities, serve the Lord and work for His use." [She left her last message to her family at her bedside] .

George, the Winn's second son, graduated in 1908 from Omaha Theological Seminary [Presbyterian Seminary in Nebraska], and became a pastor in Seoul, Korea. Julia, their second daughter, was married to Walter Erdman, who graduated from Princeton University. [Walter Erdman did not attend theological seminary, but instead took a position as assistant minister for several years, worked to promote missionaries in general, and finally became a missionary, serving in Korea for many years.]

Merle, their third son, graduated from Princeton Theological Seminary, and came to Kanazawa as a missionary. However he became seriously ill, and returned to the United States, and died the following year at the age of 37. His wife Rowena H. Winn, continued their mission work, and was assigned to Japan. For six years she taught at the Hokuriku Gakuin Junior College of Nursery Education. For three years from 1955, she was elected President of the Hokuriku Gakuin Junior College of Nursery Education.

Merle Winn, the son of Merle and Rowena Winn, decided as a young adult to return to Japan, and following his parents' wishes became a professor at Doshisha University, where he taught Japanese youth.

Appendix 1

Mrs. Winn of Japan and Manchuria

Thomas Clay Winn

We have all seen photographs of absent loved ones and thought that they were good. But never did any one see in the best photograph, the beauty of soul which shone from the dear face and eyes.

In returning home this time, I came [became] convinced that I could render no better service to those who heard me than to tell them something of the one I knew and loved the best of all.

I feel, however, that my best word-portrait will fall far short of being a true picture of the real achievements of that life of faith.

Lila C. Winn was a woman who did not know the meaning of selfishness. Such a feeling I verily believe never had a place in her heart. Her thoughts and plans were always for others. She unfailingly devoted her effort and labor to the help and good of those within her reach. She was devoted in mind and body to every good thing possible of accomplishment. And it was always the marvel of those who knew her that she could accomplish so much. She was always finding good deeds to perform where others were idle. They were idle because they did not see any thing to do, or any thing they thought they could do. Her eyes and heart instinctively saw the needs of others. And her hands and feet, impelled by love, set about supplying those needs.

As I was passing through Osaka, on my way home in May, a friend upon whom I called, then living in the house we formerly occupied, recalled to me some instances which I perhaps never thought of except as a matter of course in her life. The friend said, "I came here on an errand one day, and I found to my surprise Mrs. Winn washing and binding up the sore leg of a poor coolie she had met on the streets and persuaded to come home with her that she might thus minister to him." She also said, "I can never forget what I once witnessed in this front hall. I walked into the open door unexpectedly to Mrs. Winn and there I saw her down on her knees praying for a Japanese woman whom she had apparently been teaching, and it seemed as though she could not let the woman go until she believed on the Savior."

Her sympathy was not restricted to the lowly. Those in high and even highest circles were objects of her love, and for their best welfare her efforts were put forth. She never hesitated to seek out those who would naturally think themselves rich and in need of nothing, and try to minister to their spiritual good.

These things, which are only examples of her unremittent service rendered to others, witness to the fact that she never thought of saving her life; nor seemed to be conscious that she lost it for others' sake!

She was a diligent woman, ever working up to the limit of her physical powers. The day when she was most suddenly called away, I felt that she had literally worn herself out. Her powers had been exhausted by her incessant labors. She was never, almost literally never, known to sit down for idle chat and conversation as many of us frequently do. If not too tired, and tired she [delete: tired she] seldom acknowledged that she was, some useful work employed her busy fingers. Few persons are as unceasingly busy while engaged in social conversation, as she was. That social chat was ever made the opportunity of introducing something religious and helpful to faith and joy in the Lord. While I would be thinking out the best way of approach to a caller's heart, it often happened that she would introduce the subject in a most natural and tactful manner, so that the conversation easily turned in that direction. Religious things formed the subject upon which she could talk more easily than upon almost any other. It is what her heart was full of and out of its abundance she spoke.

When travelling to Mission Meeting one summer, we had an hour to wait at a station. When she found that out she said she wanted to call on a young man and his parents. He was sick and she would surely find them all at home. The young man, formerly her Sunday school scholar, had finished the grammar school. It was borne in upon her heart that she ought to encourage him to study for the Christian ministry. She was back on time as promised, and had made a sincere effort to help one more see his duty and privilege. Later, word came that that exhortation had enabled parents and son to dedicate his life to the Gospel ministry. Here is illustration of being zealous in season and out of season, which was unceasingly exemplified by her. Scarcely a day was allowed to pass, without trying to save or bless some souls.

She was a good Bible student and knew the Scriptures well. It was generally possible for her to turn to any passage she wished. When a girl yet in her teens, she read aloud to her grandmother whose eyes were dim, most if not all of Scott's Commentary. That exercise fixed in her memory a large amount of Bible knowledge which was ready at call for her use. Many of her explanations of Bible texts were original and elucidating. Her thoughts about the sacred Book were beautiful and instructive. These ideas expressed her experience of the truths she taught, and gave them a singular power as uttered by her. I received a series of resolutions which were passed by the W.C.T.U. ladies at their annual summer meeting this year (1913). Those resolutions ended with the statement that they were sent:

"Remembering with loving appreciation the interest Mrs. T. C. Winn always shared in the work of this society, and having felt the spiritual power she exercised over those with whom she came in contact, with special thought of the helpful devotional service," (a Bible reading). "she led here a year ago."

She was sociable and took the greatest pleasure in showing hospitality. It was done with such grace and kindliness that the most timid was won to her. Our home was a place to which all classes were welcomed and loved to come. Many have found it to be an example of a true home. It was because of the little woman who presided over her house in such a Christ-like spirit.

Just one month after we had laid the dear form away to await the resurrection, a young lady missionary on her way to Chefoo called at my door and asked if Mrs. Winn was at home. She said she had received the kindest care from Mrs. Winn when landing an entire stranger in Dairen [Dalian] a year or two before, and she wanted to come around with her husband to give expression to her gratitude.

Here is a tribute from the necrological report of the Council of Presbyterian and Reformed Missions:

"Without undue reflection on any one, we may still properly say that there are ideal missionary homes, ideal missionary wives, and ideal missionary mothers. The members of the council will agree that Mrs. Winn attained the ideal in a degree permitted to few; and her example, the example of the home of which she was the center, may well be a stimulus to us all to strive for the very best things and the highest."

From very early years, she was a personal worker and soul winner. After hearing of her death, a friend wrote; "Lila used to talk to me and try to get me to become a Christian when we were children together in the primary school. I think that was her life."

The mission to which she belonged made this entry upon its minutes: "Resolved, That the Mission puts on record its deep sense of loss in the death of Mrs. T. C. Winn and its appreciation of the qualities of heart and mind which made of her a missionary above our power to praise. She turned many to righteousness and she will shine as the brightness of the firmament and as the stars for ever and ever. We offer to her bereaved husband and children the heartfelt sympathy of a mission which admired and loved her, and which will never cease to remember the example she has set of a follower of

Christ who pleased not herself and was ever in her work as one who served." What follows is an extract from the Board's letter:

"Mrs. Winn was a graduate of Knox College, Galesburg, Illinois, a woman of disciplined and cultured mind, of unusual attractiveness of personality, of a nature so loving that it drew all about her into her friendship, of great skill and tact in dealing with those for whom she was working, and of such kindliness and good sense that her presence was counted a great blessing in any mission station to which she might be assigned. In Dairen and throughout Manchuria she worked with unceasing energy among the Japanese to make Christ known to them; and to win them to faith in Christ and to the joy and strength of Christian discipleship was her one absorbing endeavor."

Wherever duty took her; even in the market place and shop, among callers and trades people who came only to the door, very few who came in contact with her failed to receive some message about what was the dearest subject to her heart—the love of God for sinful men.

In my mind, these words were always associated with her, "He that roweth bountifully shall reap also bountifully." It was because she sowed beside all waters, "the good seed which is the word of God," that the things which I've quoted could be said of her by her Mission and Board.

She was unceasingly visiting homes and hospitals to carry delicacies as well as to read the Word of God and to sing hymns for the comfort and cheer of the inmates. I have a photograph taken of her as she stood beside the bicycle on which she daily went around the city to minister physical and spiritual gifts alike. She did not ride for the mental or bodily enjoyment of it, but because she was enabled by it to accomplish so much more than would otherwise have been possible. She and her bicycle were familiar objects in every part of the city.

Mrs. Winn's personality was attractive. She could gather people around her in a wonderful way and hold them while the story of salvation was presented to them. Many have been the times when I sat in my study and listened, while in another part of the house she kept a room full of women convulsed with laughter at her witticisms as she was demonstrating something in cooking or fancy work. This was only preparatory to teaching them the Bible lesson she had chosen for the day. At her funeral a man representing one of the groups of Christians in the country spoke of this fact. He said it had impressed itself upon his mind. At times, he remarked, it was difficult to understand what she said, (she was not what is called a good speaker of Japanese), but yet people would gather to hear her. "If I should talk in that way," he said, "people would run away from me. Instead of being attracted they would be repelled; and yet they would gladly come to hear her."

Here let it be added, that in an emergency she could be relied upon to take charge of almost any kind of service that might be lacking a leader. She was seldom at a loss for a Bible subject upon which to speak, but in a marked degree, verified the Savior's words: "He that believeth on me, from within him shall flow rivers of living water."

In her work she was resourceful. She was not restricted to set ways of doing things, but was inventive of new methods. Moreover there was little in the way of womanly accomplishments at which she was not an adept. Our children's clothes were most of them her handiwork. All four of them were fitted by her for the High School before they returned to this country to complete their education. The forenoons were given to their class room work, while the afternoons were devoted to such activities as I have hinted at.

During the last two years of her life we were more than ever engaged in touring together. May I give you an idea of how she spent her time on one of those tours? The first place at which we stopped would be thirty to sixty miles away. Arriving there, two or three meetings were the order; one for women, one for children and the third for a mixed audience of men and women.

Alighting from the train, the dear woman would begin her activities at once. Calls were made to invite people to the meetings. Things were bought, by herself often, for the cooking class. If no cooking class was to be held, the time on the cars had been occupied by making sample pieces of knitting or crocheting which the class was to be taught. She did this kind of work which taxed her physically, because she believed a knowledge of these things added to the comfort of families, (and we had proof of it), and because by teaching them, many women were reached who would not be in any other way. After a most strenuous hour or hour and a half at the woman's meeting, she would hasten to the children's class—a Sunday school on a week day. To these children her best efforts would be given in teaching them Bible verses and hymns. Her aim with children was to get them to memorize Bible texts and hymns; fully believing that truth thus implanted in the heart would bring forth fruit in the life. At the end of these two meetings there were generally some who were called upon, in order to teach or exhort them. Then came our supper, consisting of what our lunch baskets supplied. Before time for the evening meeting, a few minutes were snatched for rest. At the preaching service her duty was to take care of the music. Generally the day closed with a social time when religious and other subjects were talked over. To reach the next place on our journey might require an all night's ride on the cars, or only until two or three hours past midnight. In the latter case the journey would be interrupted and a pallet on the floor in a Japanese house would be sought, where the night's rest would be finished. This program with some variation was followed from Monday till Saturday, twice a month. In all these experiences and circumstances her spirit was serene and sweet. Her heart overflowed with gladness because these things could be done in Jesus' Name.

This highest of all purposes had absolute mastery of her affections and powers; and all she had was consecrated to it.

She could say, "This one thing I do." And it required a very serious thing to prove a hindrance or interruption of what she had planned to attempt. Moreover, she never acknowledged defeat. If others thought her worsted she would not believe it. If insurmountable difficulties rose to block her way, she would, so to speak, calmly walk around them and proceed unperturbed on her course.

When a little girl she had made up her mind to be a missionary to the heathen. But she thought that being a missionary involved being burned at the stake. I have heard her happy laugh at the ludicrousness of her childhood thoughts, as she told me that she used to open the door of her mother's heated oven and put her hand in and hold it there to see if should endure the pain of being burned alive! But notwithstanding her belief as to what it meant, she was not moved from her determination to be a missionary.

Once she was attacked by a painful eye disease. The doctor came to treat her and found it necessary to tightly bandage her eyes and shut out all the light for a time. During those days we supposed of course she would rest and be quiet at home. But no such thought was hers, and meet her engagements she would! She had a jinrikisha called, and to the coolie who pulled it she entrusted herself, while she directed him where to take her. In this way she conducted meetings, and went about calling from house to house, probably. At two different times she was seriously hurt upon the streets of Osaka by collision with rapidly moving jinrikishas. Both times the family doctor put her to bed, but she refused to stay there and went on with her service to which love constrained her, enduring much suffering the while.

Since she has gone, the many, many letters of condolence that came from Europeans, and the sayings of the Japanese, agreed in showing the very highest regard for her: "Thank you very much for writing about Mrs. Winn's falling asleep. It was not a bit like death, was it? Just like a child who has grown so tired and weary, holding out to the last ounce of strength and then giving up without a struggle, and being carried off to sleep and rest. One does not sorrow deeply for Mrs. Winn. We are just glad that her reward was so great, her home-going was so painless, her coronation so gloriously victorious."

"Her life has been a constant inspiration to me, and when I have been tired and tempted, and when I have been disappointed in my fellow workers and have all but thought the effort was not worth while, times and times without number Mrs. Winn's beautiful life of unswerving and of untiring devotion has come to my mind, and I have been helped to go on in the struggle."

"One of the pleasantest recollections of my editorship of the 'Messenger' (a little paper in Japan) is the reception of a couple of manuscripts from Mrs. Winn's pen. They were so clearly expressed, so beautifully written and evidently the expression of a devout and consecrated spirit, that they made a strong impression upon me as they passed through my hands."

"The funeral of Mrs. Winn taught me it was time for us not to think of limitations, but of possibilities. Her strong faith, her power in prayer, her quietness of spirit, even under the most provoking circumstances, the multitude of souls she won for the Master, all say: 'There are no limitations to one of her faith and consecration!'"

And now I am sure you will want to listen to some tributes from the Japanese. This is from a young woman to whom a very real service had been rendered:

"This evening when I came back from a meeting, Miss Smith called me to her study and with a pale look she told me that she had a very sad news. But how could I dream that it was such a sad, surprising one! I have never seen Mrs. Winn, yet my heart yearns her dearly. I am so sorry to think that my negligence has robbed me of the last chance to express my hearty gratitudes to her for her loving kindnesses to me and for what she has done for our people groping in the darkness. I feel though one of the shining lights of this dark world is quenched too soon."

One of our Japanese teachers said recently:

"I was traveling alone several years ago and was very hot and tired and without lunch. Mrs. Winn did not know me, yet she realized my condition and opened her lunch basket and insisted upon sharing its contents with me. Such kinds I had never before experienced nor can I forget it."

The first sense of any comfort that crept into my heart after my agonizing sorrow befell me, was in listening to what the Japanese were saying about her. I discovered that they had rightly judged her character, and they understood and appreciated her far beyond anything I had supposed was possible.

You no doubt have read of the unprecedented action of the Japanese in trying to honor her memory.

The things I am about to describe, come from their grateful feelings which were expressed with sobs and tears, as they repeatedly said: "She was a benefactor of our country; she spent her life for our people; she died for us in Manchuria."

As soon as the sad news reached Dairen, the Vice-President of the South Manchuria Railway sent me a long telegram of condolence and sorrow. A special car was sent for my use in returning to Dairen; and Christian officials were appointed to accompany me. A short funeral service was requested before her body went from Sen Kin Sai, where she laid down her life. A tent was erected for the purpose, and all the highest officials and their wives were in attendance to show their respect and grief. Most of the women had been earnestly taught the truth as it is in Jesus, and prayed for and with, by her who now lay lifeless before them.

I began the long sad journey at about 7 p.m. The Christians sang a hymn as the train moved out of the station, quite a number of them going with me to the junction, thirty-one miles away.

After leaving that place where a company met the train, I had no thought of any further demonstrations of this kind. But all through the night and early morning hours, groups of people came to mingle their tears with mine and unite their voices in prayer.

At a station sixty-five miles from Dairen, a number of friends had come out to return with me from that point. From that on, others joined the company at different places, till my private car was filled.

All that night through she had a triumphal procession. It seemed to me nothing less than that.

At Dairen, I found that committees had been appointed to look after every detail of preparation for the last sad rites, and that a very special friend of ours was the chairman of them all. Concerning everything, my own and my children's wishes were followed, and all arrangements were beautifully carried out. One of the richest men in Manchuria who had recently become a Christian, printed five hundred copies of her photograph and gave them to friends throughout that province. So that wherever I go now, I find her picture occupying the honored place in the guest room.

To our great surprise they begged to be allowed to bear the funeral expenses and make it a church or state funeral. For the non-Christian community shared in it. A representative of the Mission expressed the feeling of us all when he said it was a funeral "befitting a queen."

Later as I was about to begin the erection of a monument at her grave, they came and asked the privilege of bearing the responsibility and expenses of this labor of love, and to publish a biography of her. It has all been too wonderful for me to properly describe the love they showed for her.

This fragmentary recital is altogether inadequate to rightly set forth the life and character of which I am speaking. But, you have heard enough to convince you that the beauty of the Lord was upon her and that He established the work of her hands.

Such an outstanding fact as this life, must have had a cause. I once asked her: "Lila, how old were you when you became a Christian?" "Why," she replied, "I don't remember when I became a Christian. I think I was born a Christian." On another occasion when we were talking together of having more of the Spirit's power manifested in our work, I said, "I think you filled with the Spirit, and have always thought so. Whenever I have remembered her pleased surprise at that remark, I have been glad that I made it! I sincerely believe that like John the Baptist, she was filled with the Spirit from her birth. The secret forces which moved her heart and will, were from above. From that source she ever sought and received gracious supply.

Her prayer-life was the most real one that I ever knew.

She was an early riser, and those early hours were spent in prayer. In order to have that time for communion with her Lord, she loved to be up before others were stirring. Her prayers were not a few words hastily uttered. She waited upon the Lord. She had a prayer list of persons which she daily spread before the Lord. Whenever it was possible she went to solitary places in the woods and upon the mountains, during those early hours, with her Bible, for prayer.

Often she came back from those places where she had been apart from all others, her face transfigured almost, as she whispered to me: "I found such a nice, beautiful place this morning!"

When the evening drew near the same longing to be at prayer took her away from others. If she was sought for, she was invariably found engaged in pleading with the Almighty Father. She loved "to steal awhile away from every cumbering care, and spend the hours of setting day in humble, grateful prayer."

We are looking for explanation of this life. Jesus explained it when He said:

"If ye abide in me and my words abide in you, ask whatsoever ye will, and it shall be done unto you." "He that abideth in me and I in him, the same beareth much fruit; for apart from me ye can do nothing."

THE WOMAN'S PRESBYTERIAN BOARD OF MISSIONS
OF THE NORTHWEST

Presbyterian Offices
Room 48, 509 S Wabash Avenue, Chicago
Price, 5 cents each; 50 cents per dozen

A Note on the Appendix 1

Thomas C. Winn originally wrote this last chapter about his wife Eliza upon her death in Manchuria in 1913. It was initially composed as a report to the Woman's Presbyterian Board of Missions of the Northwest in Chicago. The original title of the article was "Mrs. Winn of Japan and Manchuria," but in its Japanese translation this title has been changed to "The Religious Life of Mrs. Winn."

Hokuriku Gakuin is the name of a Christian school in Kanazawa. In the spring of 2001, a corner of the Hesser Memorial Library Junior College was named the "Minami Collection." This collection was donated in the terms of the last will and testament of Hokuriku Gakuin's Honorary Professor Nobu Minami. The librarian of the Hesser Memorial Library coincidentally discovered the article that is now the Appendix in this volume. The author of this book was informed of this discovery, and how it happened to be included in the Minami Collection.

Rev. and Mrs. Winn arrived in 1877 as missionaries of the Board of Foreign Missions of the Presbyterian Church(North) in the United States and were involved in evangelical work in Yokohama, Hokuriku, Osaka and Manchuria. Eliza passed away in October 1912, and Thomas Winn returned to the United States for a short time in May 1913. When he returned to Galesburg, where his children lived, he was asked by the Foreign Mission Board to write the article about his wife's contribution to mission outreach. This article was probably completed by late autumn 1913 and submitted to the Board, which had it printed (numbers printed are unknown) and most likely sent out to interested individuals and organizations. Some copies must have been sent to Rev. Winn. He probably forwarded a few copies to his personal friends, as well as to Tsutomu Miyoshi, the pastor of the Dalian Church. Tsutomu Miyoshi became a Christian through the support of Rev. Winn, and later became pastor of the Fujimi-cho Church as the successor to Masahisa Uemura. Tsutomu Miyoshi donated his copy of this article with the completion of the Winn Memorial Hall (the present day Eiko-kan,) and had it translated into Japanese. His donation was made with the assitance of the President of Hokuriku Gakuin, Tetsuo Banjo.

The great grandson of Thomas Clay Winn, Thomas Charles Winn, currently residing in the state of Washington, has kindly permitted the translation of this Appendix into Japanese.

Nobuo Umezome

Appendix 2

Letter by Eliza Winn to Presbyterian Foreign Mission Board

Kanazawa, Kaga
March 12th, 1895

My dear Dr. Gillespie;

As the Orphanage is a subject of great interest to me, I desire to add a few words to Mr. Winn's letter.

In the report which was forwarded at special request, I think it was stated that one of our ulterior motives in starting the work was to prove to the native Christians that we gladly gave of our means for Christian effort.

Theretofore our charity has generally been given unknown to them, and the result has been that many of the Christian [Christians] have thought all our work was carried on at Mission expense, and that our own giving was not in the proportion we urged them to give.

They think differently now, and most all our friends are profoundly impressed by the work of the Orphanage, some of them shedding tears when they see the wonderful improvement in these beggars of a year ago.

It has always been as far as possible, from our intention to make the Orphanage anything but a private charity except as the Christians gradually help on the work or help comes from their own industry.

It is unfortunate that the proposition we made to engage the man at Mission expense who should teach the art of brush making, but it was only because the same man could be utilized for the orphans, and students without extra expense and we thought there could be no objection to combining in industrial work.

Mr. Winn has already told you what a sorrow and disappointment it has been to us to find that the Board does not approve of the Orphanage.

We had long felt the need of opening an institution of this sort, and when we read how the eminently successful missionaries, Paton and Taylor considered their orphanages one of the most important factors in their work. We could hesitate no longer even if it did require some sacrifice to furnish the necessary funds.

I should perhaps confess that last year I took time with a native helper to translate into Japanese the "Life of John Paton" but like the work in the Orphanage, it was done in addition, and not at the expense of time which should be devoted to missionary effort. I think I can truly say that I have never had opportunity to do more real missionary work, and it is the highest happiness I know, to teach the Bible to those who are eager to hear.

I do not understand your meaning when you write "Missionaries are not to be prohibited from reaching out the hand of Christian lose to the helpless...but when it comes to organized effort...the question seems a different one."

Surely it cannot mean that we have the privilege to occasionally give a little temporary relief to the passing beggar, but as soon as any thing definite is undertaken with permanent good aimed at, it must be prohibited!

Although this work was begun by missionaries of the Board should never have been able to undertake it had we not a little independent means of our own, and hence it seems as if this might be considered entirely independent work.

I entirely hope for the sake of the famishing souls 8 bodies of these little ones, that the Board can allow the work of this Orphanage to be continued.

To close it would put us in a very trying position before the whole city, and verify the jeers of those who say it cannot last long.

However we know you must look at the work from a broader standpoint than ours, and we will pray for grace to submit if an adverse decision must be made.

Sincerely yours,

Lila C. Winn

Susumu Suzuki (ed.) *The Letters of Thomas Clay Winn 1878-1908,* Hokuriku Gakuin, (Kanazawa, Japan), 1985, pp. 166-168.

Appendix 3

Letter by Eliza Winn to Presbyterian Foreign Mission Board

(Received Jan. 10, 1896)

To Dr. Gillespie

The Social Side of Missionary Life,

Since man in very clime is a social being, it necessarily follows that there is a social element in the life of a missionary. Our social duties are very different from those of society men and women. We are little concerned about the ways of fashionable society, but if we would be really efficient missionaries we should cultivate and use all the social talents with which we are endowed.

It is often said that we have not only come to preach Christianity, but to live it before these people, and this must be done by our associating with them. In our daily contact with the Japanese, we must be object-lessons illustrating the truths we teach. We are living epistles known and read of all men, and this gives a serious aspect to the social side of our work.

The social duties of a missionary must begin at his own home and in his own family. The Japanese are especially curious in regard to our home life, and if they see us considerate and agreeable these [there], it impresses them most favorably, all the more so perhaps, because of the frequent lack of such elements in their own homes.

Most of us find no difficulty in cultivating sociability in our homes and yet it sometimes happens that we become absorbed in our work or worried about it, and fall into the habit of eating our meals in silence or only answering in mono-syllables. This gives the impression to our ever observing servants that we have had a family quarrel—a conclusion most deplorable!

Our children are cut off from the society of other children and are subjected to many evil influences which seems to make it imperative for us to devote much of our time to their benefit. This should not apply to mothers only. Paternal parents should share responsibility.

They will find a romp with the children is good exercise, and they may sometimes indulge in it with safety, in the place of a game of tennis or a spin on the wheel!

Missionary mothers often feel that their children demand all their time and strength, and they are unable to undertake anything in the way of missionary work. This is undoubtedly true in some cases, but none of us can tell how much out side work we can do until we make the effort. It does seem to me that the social influence of mothers in their own houses is greatly augmented when they take an active part in missionary work. Moreover it is such an entire change to go to a woman's meeting or Bible class that it is a kind of recreation, and we will come home to our families feeling better spiritually as well as physically.

When we undertake any direct missionary effort, the reflex influence upon our own children is most beneficial. Their sympathies are easily enlisted and they become very much interested in our work especially if we take pains to tell them the interesting little incidents which may have occurred at our meetings.

Our social attitude toward our servants is worth our consideration.

While it is not probably wise to devote much time to their entertainment, or especially to make a confident of any one of them. Yet if we show a real interest in their welfare we can easily gain their confidence and goodwill which will be a great advantage to us in every way. Our ways are doubtless very queer and often incomprehensible to them and it seems to me we should be very careful not to give them a wrong impression of our motives.

If at any time there is danger of their misunderstanding our actions it is well worth our while to make some explanation especially on the subject of family discipline.

We must bear in mind the social inclinations of our servants, especially if they see in us anything which they think is inconsistent with our teaching. It is emphatically true in this country that what we do in the secrecy of our own houses is known from the house tops.

When several missionary families are residing at the same station it does great good to occasionally meet together for a real frolic, on the principle that all work and no play makes Jack a dull boy.

Literary or musical evenings as well as foreign prayer meetings are also to be heartily commended. These social gatherings must tend toward uniting our hearts and bringing us into closer sympathy with each other.

A crucial test of our ability to set forth the spirit of Christ in social contact with the people comes when taking a trip into the country, or traveling on a coast steamer.

I think one is excusable for not being in exuberant spirits on a little dirty tub of a steamer, where the passengers are packed away like sardines in a box.

The surroundings are not conducive to a pleasant state of mind. Neither does it help ones feelings if he happens to be aroused from a troubled nap, by finding a man in the row next above on the floor is warming his bare feet under your pillow. But even under such annoying circumstances let us remember that any show of selfishness impatience or irritability does not fail to detract from our influence for good. I once knew of a Japanese who was traveling some distance on the same steamer with a lady missionary. They had never seen each other before, but hearing that she was a missionary, the Japanese determined to watch her by the way to see if Christianity really did make any difference in the lives of its followers. Most fortunately this young woman unwillingly bore the inspection well. She bore the discomfort and fatigue of the journey in a peasant spirit and showed a thoughtful interest in others which won the admiration of her inspector and if I mistake not the man was so impressed that he afterward studied the Truth and became a Christian himself.

On another occasion when traveling on a very crowded car, a missionary of our own Board arose and gave his seat to a Japanese woman who would otherwise have been obliged to stand. It was interesting to watch the effect of that little act of courtesy upon our fellow passengers, and presently a well dressed man came forward and begged our missionary to take his place.

Japanese callers are sometimes tedious. It requires a great deal of grace to lay aside the work we want to finish, and instead entertain a caller who seems unlimited in his hours of leisure. Circumstances alter cases, and it may not always be necessary for us to devote as much time to our caller as they would choose. Yet if we are considerate and kind in our conversation with them we gain a influence we can ill afford to lose.

The more we are in danger of being annoyed at the length of our call, let us the more earnestly teach our guest of Christ, and if we can succeed in influencing him we shall never regret the time which we have spent with him.

One can spend a great deal of time in calling upon the Japanese, and I think it pays well. A great many informal calls can be made on a single afternoon, when one simply sits at the door way for a little visit. This avoids the bother of taking off shoes and also prevents the family from giving tea and cakes.

If any of the Christians are absent from Sabbath services for several weeks, it is a good plan I think to call and inquire the cause. If they are ill, it is sometimes brings about a pleasant state of feelings to take them a little bread or ice cream. It is astonishing what affect a dish of ice cream will have on almost any of the Japanese, and I never knew any ill to result from giving it. It is quite generally known in

Kanazawa that we make ice cream for the sick, and requests some-times come for it from entire strangers. With ice cream to open the way we are welcome in almost any home and thus our circle of ac-quaintances is gradually enlarged and our influence too I hope.

There are many little kind attentions which one may pay to the suffering, which will be highly appreciated.

A music box gives a great deal of pleasure in a sick room.

Last week, the widow of a former high Government official, while calling here, said with tears in her eyes that our music box had been the chief comfort of her husband during his last illness. Bound vol-umes of illustrated papers can do the same kind of missionary ser-vice, and if one keeps a few feather pillows to soften the beds of the dying, which we give in the name of Him who had not [no] where to lay His head, may it not be one of the little deeds which we are promised shall not lose its reward! Let us show that we do not con-sider our things too nice to use in reaching the people.

Let us include our possessions when we offer ourselves up as liv-ing sacrifices which is our reasonable service.

Entertaining Japanese company often costs a good deal in times and money, but it affords much real pleasure to guests and entertain-ers, and is I think in accordance with the teaching and example of our Lord. One so often has occasion to fulfil the command to call the poor, lame, or blind, and how they do enjoy a good full meal!

If it be true at home, that the most successful way to reach a gen-tleman's purse for the missionary cause, is through a good supper at a church social, it is equally true that one may have, on some occa-sions, ulterior motives for giving a good supper here, and he is very apt to succeed in them too.

I never knew a Japanese to be ill-humored or contrary after a pleasant visit at the supper table, and if one wishes to further plans that he fears may meet with opposition. I advise him to try giving a good meal first. Moreover if there be any one, who reasonably or otherwise bears a grudge against you, his feelings will be wonderfully mollified by a dish of hot soup with "more to follow."

I speak from experience. Hot soup is more comfortable to take, those hot coals on the head! We often invite officials or prominent citizens to dinner for the sake of getting their good will and with the desire of gaining an influence over them. Many people of this class will lose their prejudice against foreigners when they are thus brought into contact with us, and will be very friendly even when they cannot be persuaded to accept of [delete: of] Christianity.

Perhaps more of them are convinced of its truth than we now know.

Let us be given to hospitality and we shall have opportunity to sow our seed by all waters.

In all our social dealing and with the Japanese, the one thing needful is a genuine interest in them and a sincere desire to do them good. Without this motive we shall surely fail to influence them even if our language and pronunciation were faultless. We must make them feel we love them if we would teach them to love Christ.

In conclusion I would remind you of the words given to us by St. Paul.

"But to do good and to communicate forget not, for with such sacrifices God is well pleased—"

Mrs. T. C. Winn
Kanazawa

Susumu Suzuki (ed.) *The Letters of Thomas Clay Winn 1878-1908*, Hokuriku Gakuin (Kanazawa, Japan), 1985, pp. 172-177.

Notes

Chapter 1

(1) Earnest E. Calkins: *They Broke the Prairie*, Greenwood Press, 1937, p. 207 & *The Encyclopedia Americana*, 1963 ed. Vol. 19, 1963, p. 40.

(2) Katsuhiro Shimizu: *America Shubetsu Bunka Jiten* (Cultural Dictionary of American States) Meicho Fukyukai, 1986, p. 153.

(3) *Dictionary of American Biography*, vol. 10, ed. By Dumas Malone, Charles Scribner's Sons, 1936, pp. 231-42.

(4) Earnest E. Calkins: ibid., p. 45.

Chapter 2

(1) Mary B. Norton et al.: *A People and a Nation*, 2nd ed. Vol. 1, Houghton Mifflin Co., 1986, p. 326.

(2) Masatoshi Ogasawara: Kyokai Shi No.2 (History of Churches), Nihon Kirisuto Kyodan Shuppan-kyoku. 1974, pp. 173-75.

Chapter 3

(1) Earnest E. Calkins: ibid., p. 45.

(2) Hiroshi Kume: *Kirisutokyo Sono Shiso to Rekishi* (Thoughts and History of Christianity), Shinyo-sha, 1993, pp. 203-15.

(3) *"1560 The Scottish Confession, Preface"* Translated by Tatsu Shishido, *Carl Barth's Works.* Vol. 9, Shinkyo Shuppan-sha, 1971, p. 8.

Chapter 4

(1) Mary B. Norton et al.: ibid., p. 277.

Chapter 5

(1) "1560 The Scottsih Confession, Preface": ibid., p. 27.

(2) Hakuyo Shibata: *Winn Fujin-den* (The Life of Mrs. Winn), Dairen Nihon Kirisutokyo Fujinkai, 1913, pp. 4-5.

Chapter 6

(1) Satoru Umene (ed.) *Sekai Kyoiku-shi Taikei 17 America Kyoiku-shi* (History of World's Education 17, History of American Education) Kodan-sha, 1975, p. 110.

(2) Paul Johnson: *A History of the American People*, Harper Perennial, 1997, pp. 471-472.

Chapter 7

(1) Harriet Beecher Stowe: *Uncle Tom's Cabin*, Library of America Paperback Classics, 2010, pp. 451-452.

(2) Henry Graff: *The Free and the Brave ~ The Story of the American People* (Teacher's Edition, Annotated), Rand McNally & Company, 1967, p.354. "Frederick Douglass: a slave who ran away and later became a distinguished leader of his freed people wrote about what it was like to be a slave." (p.354).

Chapter 8

(1) Albert Barnes, *Barnes' Notes on the Gospels—Luke, John*, Harper and Brothers, 1832, pp. 264-65.

(2) Jean Calvin, A Guide to Christian Faith (Translated by Nobuo Watanabe) Shinkyo Shuppansha, 1986. pp. 15-16.

(3) Jean Calvin: ibid., pp. 100-01.

(4) Jean Calvin: ibid., p. 104.

Chapter 9

(1) Mary B. Norton, et al.: ibid., p.74.

(2) Kanazawa Kyokai 110 Nenshi Hensan Iiinkai (ed.): Kanazawa Kyokai 110 Nenshi (History of 110 Years of Kanazawa Church), Kanazawa Church, 1997, p. 8.

Chapter 10

(1) This hymn made by Phoebe Brown was sang in Presbyterian and Methodist Churches in Japan. Hymn #4: *Hymnal*, The Presbyterian Board of Publication and Sabbath School Work, 1906. Also included in Hymn #55: *The Methodist Hymnal*, The Methodist Publishing House, 1939.

(2) Megumi Hara: *Sambika Sono Rekishi to Haikei* (Hymns: Its History and Background) Nihon Kirisuto Kyokai Shuppan-kyoku, 1980, pp. 214-15.

(3) Shoshichi Nakazawa: *Nihon no Shito: Thomas Winn Den* (Disciple of Ja-

pan, Life of Thomas Winn), 4th Edition, Winn Tonichi 90 Shunenkinennkai, 1967, pp. 13-14.
Translated version: Shoshichi Nakazawa: *Thomas Clay Winn—Life of an American Missionary in Early Modern Japan*, (Tr.) Komei Go, Kohro-sha, 2004.

Chapter 11
(1) Shoshichi Nakazawa: ibid., p. 28.

Chapter 12
(1) Shoshichi Nakazawa: ibid., p. 29.
(2) Yoko Mochizuki: *Hepburn no Shogai to Nihongo* (Life of Hepburn and Japanese Language), Shinchosha, 1987, pp. 9-235.
(3) Shoshichi Nakazawa: ibid., p. 31.
(4) Shoshichi Nakazawa,: ibid., p. 30.
(5) Kanazawa Kyokai 100 Nenshi Hensan Iinkai (ed.): Kanazawa Kyokai (History of 100 Years of Kanazawa Church) Kanazawa Kyokai Chorokai, 1981, p. 7.
(6) Kanazawa Kyokai 110 Nenshi Hensan Iinkai (ed.): ibid., p. 11.

Chapter 13
(1) Kanazawa Kyokai 100 Nenshi Hensan Iinkai (ed.): ibid., p.7-8.
(2) Colin Sloss and Dennis Kellehrer: "American Presbyterian Missionaries in Meiji Japan; Thomas Winn, a Reluctant Educator," Institute of Human Science, Kanazawa University of Economics, 2002, p. 33.

Chapter 14
(1) Shoshichi Nakazawa: ibid., p. 44.
(2) Minoru Ishikawa: *Sougawa Kyokai 100 Nenshi* (History of100 Years of Sougawa Church) Toyama Kashima-cho Church, 1986, p. 16.
(3) Kanazawa-shi Hensan Iinnkai (ed.): *Kanazawa Shishi Shiryo-hen 15* (Kanazawa City's History. Documents #15) Kanazawa City, 2001, p. 617.
(4) Rui Kohiyama: *America Fujin Senkyo-shi—Rainichi no Haikei to Sono Eikyo* (American Women Missionaries—The background of coming to Japan and its influence) Tokyo University Press, 1992, p. 227.

Chapter 15
(1) Susumu Suzuki (ed.), *The Letters of Thomas Clay Winn (1878-1908).*
    Hokuriku Gakuin, 1985, p. 13.
(2) Shoko Yamagishi: *Kita Nishi Nihon Shimbun* (Northern Japan Newpaper)
    Kita Nihon Shimbunsha Feb. 4, 5, 1964.
(3) Shoshichi Nakazawa: ibid., p. 47

Chapter 16
(1) Shoshichi Nakazawa: ibid., pp. 66-67.

Chapter 17
(1) *The Encyclopedia Americana*, 1968 Edition, vol. 9, Americana Corporation,
    1968, p. 672.
(2) *The Letters of Thomas Clay Winn (1878-1908)*: ibid., p. 17.
(3) Thomas T. Alexander:" A Letter to the Mission Board," January 7, 1884.(
    Microfilm preserved at Yokohama Kaiko Shiryokan (Yokohama Archives of
    History)
(4) Hokuriku Jogakko Dosokai (ed.) *Kaiho* 18 (Newsletter of Alumnae)
    Hokuriku Jogakko Dosokai, 1926, p. 9.

Chapter 18
(1) Kanazawa Kyokai 110 Nenshi Henshu Iinkai: ibid., p. 36.
(2) Yasushi Murao: *Hikoso Kyokai 80 Nenshi* (History of 80 Years of Hikoso
    Church) Kanazawa Hikoso Church, 1966, p.7.
(3) Yasushi Murao: ibid., p.7
(4) Megumi Hara: ibid., p. 261.

Chapter 19
(1) Kanazawa-shi Kyoiku Iinkai Bunka-ka (ed.): *Kanazawa-shi Bunkazai Ki-
    you 57 Kanazawa Rekishiteki Kenchiku* (Kanazawa City's Cultural Asset
    Journal 57, Kanazawa historical architecture) Kanazawa City Board of Edu-
    cation, 1986, p. 127.
(2) Shoshichi Nakazawa: *Kanazawa Nihon Kirisuto Kyokai 50 Nenshi* (50
    years History of Kanazawa Japan Christian Church) Kanazawa Nihon
    Kirisuto Kyokai, 1930, p. 154.
(3) Kanazawa Kyokai 110 Nenshi Hensan Iinkai,(ed.): ibid., p. 89.
(4) Kanazawa Kyokai 110 Nenshi Hensan Iinkai (ed.): ibid., p. 98.

(5) Kanazawa Kyokai 110 Nenshi Hensan Iinkai (ed.): ibid., pp. 114-15.

Chapter 20
(1) Shoshichi Nakazawa: ibid., pp. 72-74.
(2) *The Letters of Thomas Clay Winn (1878-1908)*: ibid., pp. 166-68.[See the Appendix 2]

Chapter 21
(1) Minoru Ishikawa: ibid., p. 23.
(2) Minioru Ishikawa: ibid., p. 24.
(3) Minoru Ishikawa: ibid., p. 21.
(4) Junko Takamizawa, *Eien no Ashioto* (Footsteps of Eternity), Shufu no To-mo-sha, 1976, p. 39.

Chapter 22
(1) Kanazawa 110 Nenshi Hensan Iinkai (ed.): ibid., p. 59.
(2) *The Letters of Thomas Clay Winn (1878-1908)* ibid., pp. 145-46.[Letter of Thomas C. Winn to John Gillespie, January 1st, 1894]

Chapter 23
(1) John G. Paton, Translated by Mrs. Winn: *Life of John Paton*, Kirisuto- kyo Shorui Kaisha, 1905, pp.131-35. Original Text: *Missionary to the New Hebrides—An Autobiography*, James Paton (ed.) Hodder and Stoughton, 1891. (Elibron Classic Series, 2005, pp. 354-355.)
(2) *The Letters of Thomas Clay Winn (1878-1908)*: ibid., p. 167.

Chapter 24
(1) Kanazawa Kyokai 110 Nenshi Hensan Iinkai (ed.): ibid., pp,. 89-90.
(2) Shoshichi Nakazawa: ibid., pp. 92-93.

Chapter 25
(1) *The Letters of Thomas Clay Winn (1878-1908)*: ibid., p.197. [The address changed: 478 Kyo Hori, Osaka, Japan.]
(2) Keiji Miyazawa: *Nihon Kirisuto Kyokai Osaka Minami Kyokai 50 Nenshi* (50 Years of Japan Christian Osaka Minami Church), Nihon Kirisuto Kyo-kai Osaka Minami Kyokai, 1935, pp. 30-31.

Chapter 26
(1) Shoshichi Nakazawa: ibid., p. 110.
(2) Hakyuyo Shibata: ibid., p. 28.
(3) Shoshichi Nakazawa: ibid., p. 110.
(4) Hakuyo Shibata: ibid., p. 31.
(5) Shoshichi Nakazawa:ibid,, 119.
(6) Shoshichi Nakazawa: ibid., p. 141.

Chapter 27
(1) Shoshichi Nakazawa: ibid., p. 132-34.
(2) Shoshichi Nakazawa: ibid., pp. 134-35.
(3) Shoshichi Nakazawa: ibid., p. 144.

[Quotations from the Bible: *The Holy Bible:* Revised Standard Version, British and Foreign Bible Societies, Published by Collins Bible: A division of Harper-Collins Publishers]

Appendixes
(1) Thomas C. Winn: "Mrs. Winn of Japan and Manchuria"; A Report to the Mission Board of Presbyterian Church in the U.S.A. (North)., 1913 [Published by The Woman's Presbyterian Board of Missions of the Northwest: Room 48, 409 S. Wabash Avenue, Chicago, U.S.A. Price: 5 cents each; 50 cents per dozen.]
(2) Letter by Eliza Winn to Presbyterian Foreign Mission Board (March 12, 1895) *The Letters of Thomas Clay Winn (1878-1908)*, Susumu Suzuki (ed.) Hokuriku Gakuin, 1985, pp. 166-168.
(3) Letter by Eliza Winn to Presbyterian Foreign Mission Board (received Jan. 10, 1896). *The Letters of Thomas Clay Winn (1878-1908)*: ibid., pp. 172-177.

193

Acknowledgments

This book was written as a product of writing an article "Mary Hesser: A Pioneer in Girls' Education."

Mary Hesser was the founder of Kanazawa Girls' School which later became Hokuriku Gakuin, but actually Eliza Winn was the original planner of this institution.

The author was inspired greatly when knowing the religious life of Eliza Winn, and this led to compiling this book, but I offer a prayer of gratitude to God for giving me opportunity to share this history.

I would like to express acknowledgments to the following references which I have used in this book.

(1) *The Letters of Thomas Clay. Winn*, Susumu Suzuki (ed.), Hokuriku Gakuin, 1985
(2) *They Broke the Prairie*, Earnest E. Calkins, Greenwood Press, 1937.
(3) *Dictionary of American Biography,* 10 vols. Edited by Allen Johnson, Charles Scribner's Sons, 1927.
(4) *Life of John Paton*, Translated by Eliza Winn, Kiristuokyo Shorui Kaisha, 1905.
(5) *Winn Fujin-den* (The Life of Mrs. Winn), Hakuyo Shibata, Dairen Kiristutokyo Fujinkai, 1913.
(6) *Nihon no Shito: Thomas Winn Den* (Disciple of Japan: Life of Thomas C. Winn) Shoshichi Nakazawa, 1967.
(7) *Kanazawa Kyokai 110 Nen Shi* (History of 110 Years of Kanazawa Church) ed. Kanazawa Kyokai Editorial Committee, Kanazawa Church Session, 1997.
(8) *Kanazawa Kyokai 100 Nen Shi* (History of 100 Years of Kanazawa Church) ed. Kanazawa Kyokai Editorial Com-

mittee, Kanazawa Church Session, 1981.

(9) *Kanazawa Hikoso Kyokai 80 Nen Shi* (History of 80 Years of Kanazawa Hikoso Church) Kanazawa Hikoso Church, 1906.

(10) *Sougawa Kyokai 100 Nen Shi* (History of 100 years of Sougawa Church) Minoru Ishikawa, Toyama Kashima-cho Church, 1986.

I would like to express much appreciation especially to Hokuriku Gakuin Junior College's Hesser Memorial Library, Sugiyama Women's Nisshin Library, Kanazawa Municipal Library, Ishikawa International Information Library, and also to Galesburg First Presbyterian Church's Elder's Association for looking into the materials.

In this book, I have rewritten old style Japanese into modern style, but in doing so Issei Aisaka of Kanazawa Church has proof read the manuscript and Nobuko Hosokawa has gone through and edited this book and I also thank Yoshinobu Mita for correcting into proper Japanese.

Most of all I extend my greatest appreciation to Kanazawa Church Session not to let original edition be out of print but decided to print this new edition.

Nobuo Umezome

Picture Credits

1. Eliza Caroline Winn and Thomas Clay Winn:
   Shoshichi Nakazawa: *Thomas Clay Winn~The Life of an American Missionary in Early Modern Japan,* Translated by Komei Go, Kohro-sha, 2004 (Photography Pages, p.2.) Cover page (1).
2. The Winn family, circa 1888: (ibid., p.7.) Cover page(2).
3. The Winn family: (ibid., p.6.) Cover page (3).
4. Silas Willard: [https://www.findagrave.com/memorial/a5579915/silas-willard] p.2.
5. Cordelia Chambers Willard: [Copyright of photo: Special Collections and Archives, Knox College Library, Galesburg, Illinois, U.S.A.] p. 2.
6. Matthew Chambers and Hannah Smith Chambers, [https://www.findagrave.com/memorial], p.3.
7. Knox College which Eliza attended
   Nobuo Umezome: *Shinko no Shonin~ Eliza Winn den* (Witness of Faith~The Life of Eliza Winn) Kanazawa Church, 2007, (Photography Page p.2.) p. 12.
8. House built by Eliza's father (Data sent by Julia Pollock) p. 21.
9. Eliza in teens (Data sent by Thomas Charles Winn) p. 23.
10. Double Wedding (Data sent by Thomas Charles Winn) p. 51.
11. Samuel R. Brown [Copyright of photo: Yokohama Archives of History] p. 56.
12. D. James Curtis Hepburn [Copyright of photo: Yokohama Archives of History] p. 58.
13. Early members of Kanazawa Church, 1882
    Shoshichi Nakazawa, ibid., (Photography Page p.4), p. 71.
14. First church building at Otemachi 2 banchi. Also used as Aishin School.

Shoshichi Nakazawa, ibid., (Photography Page, p. 4), p. 75.
15. Mary Hesser
Hokuriku Gakuin Rekishi Monogatari (Historical Story of Hokuriku Gakuin), Hokuriku Gakuin Historical Archives, 2017, p. 10. p. 93.
16. Kanazawa Girls' School at Kamikakibatake (ibid., p.28.) p. 95.
17. Organ played by Eliza Winn at the Opening Ceremony of Kanazawa Girls' School,(ibid., p. 8.), p.96.
18. First students and staffs of Kanazawa Girls' School, (ibid. p. 11.), p.96.
19. Chuei Aoki, first pastor of the Kanazawa Church
Kanazawa Kyokai Hyakunenshi (100th Anniversary of Kanazawa Church, Nihon Kirisuto Kyodan Kanazawa Kyokai Hyakunenshi Hensan Iinkai, 1981, (Photography Page p.4.), p. 99.
20. Kanazawa Foreign Mission Station: Shoshichi Nakazawa, ibid., (Photography page p. 5.), p. 103.
21. John G. Paton
John G. Paton, Missionary to the New Hebrides~ An Autobiography, D. James Paton, Hodder and Stoughton, London, 1891. (Elibron Classics Series 2005, (Front Page), p.127.
22. Grave of Eliza Winn
"Mrs Winn of Japan and Manchuria," Thomas Clay Winn, The Woman's Presbyterian Board of Missions of the Northeast, 1913, (Last Page), p.155.

Maps and Chart

Map of New Hebrides: *Letters and Sketches from the New Hebrides,*
Maggie Whitecross Paton (Mrs. John G. Paton), ed. Rev. J. A. S. Paton, London: Hodder and Stroughton, 1894, 2nd ed., p. 29. (Biblio-
life: Enlarge Print Edition), p. 132.

[Following maps and chart: Illustrated by Toshitaka Takei, graduate
of Kyoto Seika University]
1. Route Winn's group took from Yokohama to Kanazawa: September 23-October 4, 1879, p.64.
2. Map of Kaga han (fief), p.65.
3. Map of Hokuriku District: Related Places of Winn's Mission, p.
   81.
4. Historical Map of Kanazawa Church, p. 204.
5. Map of Main Places Eliza and Thomas C. Winn Stayed and Traveled, p. 205.
6. Historical Chart of Hokuriku Gakuin School System, pp. 206~207.

198

Index

206

Historical Map of Kanazawa Church

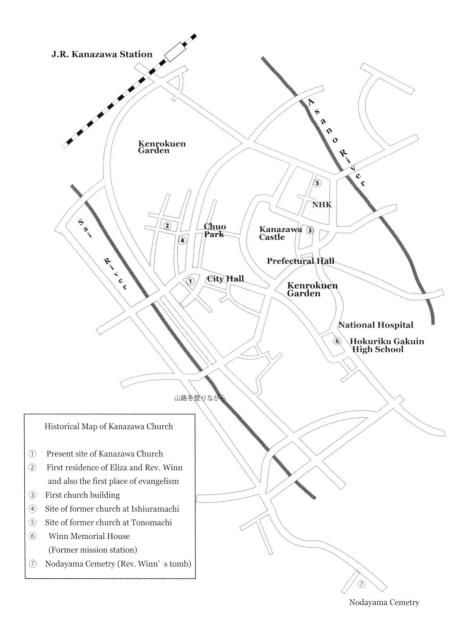

J.R. Kanazawa Station

Kenrokuen Garden

Asano River

Sai River

NHK

Chuo Park

Kanazawa Castle ③

② ④

Prefectural Hall

① City Hall

Kenrokuen Garden

National Hospital

⑥ Hokuriku Gakuin High School

山路を登りながら

Historical Map of Kanazawa Church

① Present site of Kanazawa Church
② First residence of Eliza and Rev. Winn
   and also the first place of evangelism
③ First church building
④ Site of former church at Ishiuramachi
⑤ Site of former church at Tonomachi
⑥ Winn Memorial House
   (Former mission station)
⑦ Nodayama Cemetry (Rev. Winn's tomb)

⑦

Nodayama Cemetry

Map of Main Places Eliza and Thomas C. Winn Stayed and Traveled

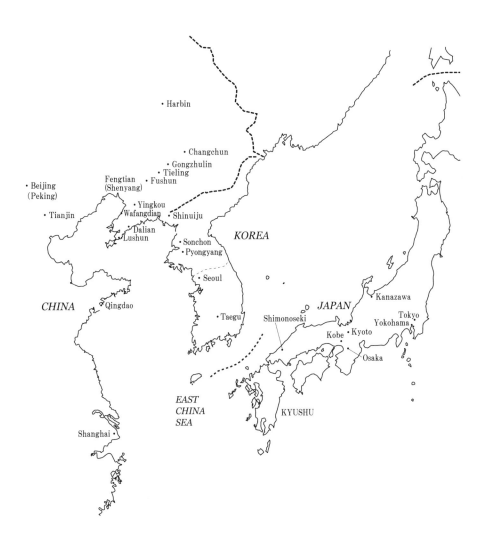

· Harbin

· Changchun
· Gongzhulin
· Tieling
Fengtian · Fushun
(Shenyang)
· Beijing
(Peking)
· Yingkou
· Tianjin   Wafangdian
· Shinuiju
Dalian
Lushun
· Sonchon   *KOREA*
· Pyongyang

· Seoul

CHINA   Qingdao
Kanazawa
· Taegu   *JAPAN*
Shimonoseki   Tokyo
Yokohama
Kobe · Kyoto
Osaka

*EAST
CHINA
SEA*   *KYUSHU*

Shanghai ·

Historical Chart Of Hokuriku Gakuin School System

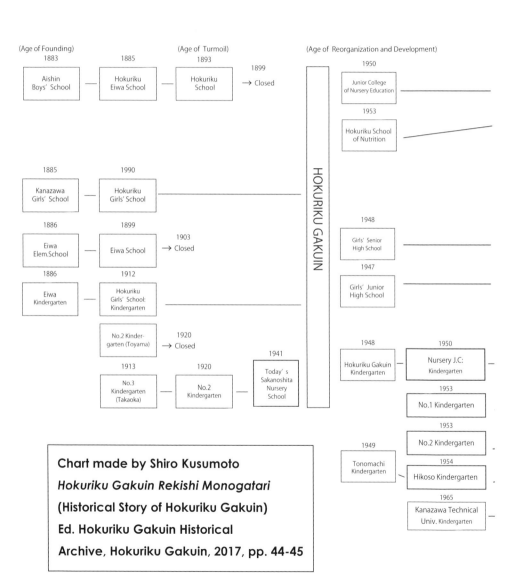

(Age of Founding)

(Age of Turmoil)

(Age of Reorganization and Development)

HOKURIKU GAKUIN

1883 — Aishin Boys' School
1885 — Hokuriku Eiwa School
1893 — Hokuriku School
1899 → Closed
1950 — Junior College of Nursery Education
1953 — Hokuriku School of Nutrition

1885 — Kanazawa Girls' School
1990 — Hokuriku Girls' School

1886 — Eiwa Elem.School
1899 — Eiwa School
1903 → Closed
1948 — Girls' Senior High School
1947 — Girls' Junior High School

1886 — Eiwa Kindergarten
1912 — Hokuriku Girls' School: Kindergarten

No.2 Kindergarten (Toyama)
1920 → Closed

1913 — No.3 Kindergarten (Takaoka)
1920 — No.2 Kindergarten
1941 — Today's Sakanoshita Nursery School

1948 — Hokuriku Gakuin Kindergarten
1950 — Nursery J.C: Kindergarten
1953 — No.1 Kindergarten
1953 — No.2 Kindergarten

1949 — Tonomachi Kindergarten
1954 — Hikoso Kindergarten

1965 — Kanazawa Technical Univ. Kindergarten

Chart made by Shiro Kusumoto
Hokuriku Gakuin Rekishi Monogatari
(Historical Story of Hokuriku Gakuin)
Ed. Hokuriku Gakuin Historical
Archive, Hokuriku Gakuin, 2017, pp. 44-45

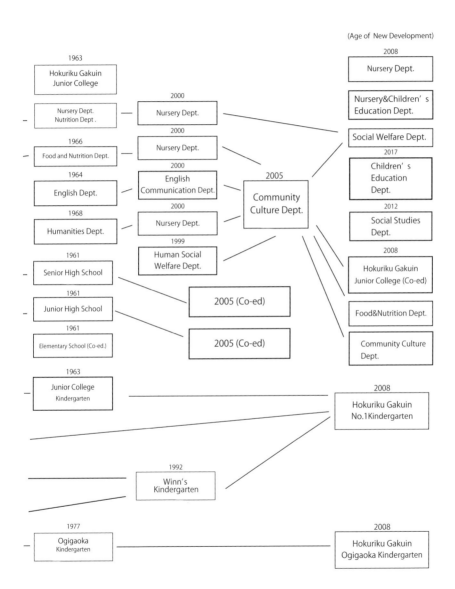

(Age of New Development)

A timeline of significant events
in the life of Eliza Caroline Winn

1853	May 1	Eliza Willard born in Galesburg, Illinois as third daughter of Silas and Cordelia Willard
		Matthew Chambers Willard (1843-1894) brother
		Frances Cordelia Willard (1847-1934) sister
		Emma Almira Willard (1851-1906) sister
1854		Railroad reaches to Galesburg and on to Mississippi River
1857		Eliza's father Silas Willard passes away
1860-1867		Enters elementary school in Galesburg
1861-1864		Civil War
1867-1870		Attends high school in Galesburg
1870		Enters Knox College
1874		Graduates from Knox College
1875		Studies one extra year at Knox College
1877	Sept.20	Eliza marries with Thomas Clay Winn. Double ceremony with her sister Emma Almira
1877	Dec.26	Thomas and Eliza arrive in Yokohama, Japan abroad SS City of Peking
1878	Aug. 9	Mary, the Winn's first child is born in Yokohama
1879	Oct. 4	The Winns arrive at Kanazawa
1879	Nov.15	Willard, their first son is born in Kanazawa
1881	May	Founding of Kanazawa Church
1882	July 14	George, their second son is born in Kanazawa
1882	Aug. 1	Willard passes away
1885	Mar. 23	Julia, their second daughter is born in Kanazawa

1885	Sept. 9	Opening ceremony of Kanazawa Girls' School takes place
1886	Apr.	The Winns return to U.S.A. to seek treatment for Thomas' damaged eye
1887		The Winns return to Japan
1890	Aug. 28	Merle, their third son is born in Kanazawa
1892		Eliza opens an orphanage in Kanazawa for 9 years
1897		The Winns spend a year in the U.S.A.
1898	Sept.	The Winns move to Osaka
1905		Eliza publishes *Life of John Paton* in Japanese
1906	Sept.	The Winns relocate to Dalian, Manchuria to minister to Japanese citizens there
1912	Oct. 8	Eliza dies one week after relocating from Dalian to Qianjinzhai,Manchuria
1912	Oct. 12	Funeral of Eliza Winn is held
1913	May 3	Dedication of Memorial to Eliza at Xiwangjiatun, Manchuria
1925		Mary dies of cancer
1928		Merle dies of heart disease
1931	Feb. 8	Thomas Clay Winn dies in Kanazawa

Profiles

Author: Nobuo Umezome

Nobuo Umezome was born in 1929. He graduated from Aoyama Gakuin University's College of Literature, Theology Course. He taught English at Toyama Prefectural High schools, and later became English professor at Hokuriku Gakuin Junior College in Kanazawa. He has been an Elder of Kanazawa Church which Thomas and Eliza Winn founded. He wrote an article on Mary Hesser, the first head of Hokuriku Gakuin, but discovered that Eliza Winn was the original planner and a great supporter of the Girls' School in Kanazawa. He has written a book on Thomas Clay Winn and has compiled Rev. Winn's sermons included in the book *Thomas Winn Senkyoshi: Denki to Sekkyo* (Rev. Thomas Winn ~ His Life and Sermons), Hokuriku Gakuin, 2018. Also he is the author of *Sambika Monogatari* (Stories on Hymnals) I~III, Shinkyo Shuppan-sha, 1992-94. Presently, after his retirement, he serves as the Director of Winn's Memorial Hall (Hokuriku Gakuin Historical Archives).

* For more information on Winn's Memorial Hall, please contact:
  Ms Etsuko Yamamoto
  Hokuriku Gakuin: Winn Memorial Hall
  1-10 Tobiume-cho, Kanazawa 930-8563 Japan

Translator: Komei Kure

Komei was born in 1946 in Okayama, Japan. He graduated from Canadian Academy High School in Kobe, Japan. He studied at Cornell College, Iowa (B.A. in Chemistry). Then he graduated from Kyoto University, Graduate School of Faculty of Education. He taught at Kyoto Seika University for forty years. Now he is retired and lives in Tokyo, Japan. Presently he is involved in the project of

Recording Oral History of Overseas Chinese in Western Japan. He has published *Kobe: City of Lights* (Ed. David Rahn and Emi Higashiyama) Kobe Shimbun Publishing Center Co. Ltd., 2013.

Editor: David Philip Rahn

David was born in Elgin, Illinois on October 10, 1946. His parents started working as Christian missionaries at Toyonaka Church in Japan in 1953. He attended Canadian Academy, and then studied at Cornell College, Iowa. He was active as President of Public Affairs Club at Cornell and majored in History. He studied Japanese History at the University of Michigan and gained Master's degrees in East Asian Studies and History. Later he earned Master of Divinity degree at Iliff School of Theology in Colorado. David began serving as United Methodist Minister and lived in Grand Blanc, Michigan. David completed Master of Social Work degree at the University of Michigan. While working full-time as a social worker, David continued to minister, delivering sermons to rural Michigan congregations on Sunday morning.

He passed away on July 17, 2020, and in his obituary is stated as follows:

"Dave's early experiences bridging cultures and surviving a serious illness, combined with his naturally observant character, shaped a lifetime of wry and generous observation and care that would eventually interconnect in ministry, and hospice social work, and mental health counseling. … As a social worker, Dave's spiritual training, powers of observation, and profound empathy were perfectly suited to his work. He cared for his patients with warmth and sensitivity, and formed lifelong friendship with his coworkers."

David has also edited Shoshichi Nakazawa: *Thomas Clay Winn~The Life of an American Missionary in Early Modern Japan*, Kohro-sha, 2004.

Editor: Thomas Charles Winn

Tom was born in Guatemala, C.A. in 1945 where his parents were assigned to establish Laubach literacy centers. Tom's father, Paul R. Winn was the grandson of Thomas Clay and Eliza Willard Winn. Paul's father George H. Winn, became a missionary to Korea. Tom's parents were moved to Colombia, S.A. then to Japan where they were professors in Meiji Gakuin in Tokyo then several universities in Kyoto. While living in Tokyo Tom attended American School in Japan (ASIJ), then Canadian Academy in Kobe where David and Komei were classmates. Tom attended Seattle Pacific College then graduated from Western Washington University followed by attaining a Master's Degree in Education from Leslie College. Tom taught reading and computer science in the La Conner Public School. He loved hiking, mountain climbing, skiing, and sailing. The summer of 1963 Tom and Komei walked Tokaido Road which was the historical trade route from Kyoto, the ancient capital, to Tokyo the modern capitol. In October 2018 Tom and his wife Mary walked along the Nakasendo Road from Ena to Tokyo. He passed away in the spring of 2019. Surviving are his wife, Mary, and daughters from a previous marriage, Jennifer Winn Faley and Stacy Winn Brown.

Special thanks:

Julia Winn Pollock, sister of Thomas Charles Winn has helped greatly in proof reading the text of Eliza Winn's Book. She has studied at Canadian Academy in Kobe, Japan. She went to West Virginia University and has undergraduate degree in Sociology. Then, she received Master's Arts in Teaching from Mary Baldwin College. She is certified to teach Japanese in the state of Virginia. Now she lives in Topsail Beach, North Carolina. She has sent valuable materials including photos and family information related to Eliza Winn and helped financing in the publication of this book.

Mark Meyer is son of Elizabeth Winn Meyer, Thomas Charles

Winn's elder sister. He is a doctor in family practice. His family lives near Pittsburg and makes regular trips to Honduras to establish and help run a clinic in a small town that was devastated by a hurricane. It was Meyer's family who encouraged to publish the Life of Eliza Winn. He has attended Winn and Willard family Reunion in spring of 2019 at "The Great House" where Eliza Winn grew up, which is now preserved as a Guest House.

Contacts:

For inquiries on purchase of the book or any other matters, please contact the following e-mail addresses.

Komei Kure (Japan): njwxd152@yahoo.co.jp

Julia Winn Pollock (U.S.A.): jawp2@me.com

Witness of Faith ~ The Life of Eliza Winn

発行日：2020 年 12 月 15 日
編　者：梅染信夫
訳　者：呉宏明
編　集：デイビッド・ラン
　　　　トーマス・チャールズ・ウィン
発行者：相坂一
　　（株）松籟社
　　〒612-0801　京都市伏見区深草正覚町 1-34
　　電話：075-531-2878
　　FAX：075-532-2309

装幀：多田昭彦
印刷・製本：亜細亜印刷株式会社

Published: December 15, 2020
Author: Nobuo Umezome
Translated by Komei Kure
Edited by David Rahn and Thomas Charles Winn
Publisher: Hajime Aisaka
Shoraisha Co., Ltd.
1-34 Shokakucho, Fushimiku, Kyoto
612-0801 Japan
Tel: 075-531-2878
Fax: 075-532-2309
Cover and Jacket: Designed by Akihiko Tada
Printed by Asia Printing Office Corporation

ISBN 978-4-87984-396-8
C0023
定価はカバーに表示しています。